Ask Your Angel Guides

"Susan Browne's new book, *Ask Your Angel Guides*, is a must-have, especially if you want your life to run more smoothly and happily. Every page is filled with reminders, information, exercises, and visualizations. Whether you want to overcome bad habits, heal family relationships, manifest something special, or create good boundaries, Susan Browne explains how the angels can help you. She also introduces dragons, unicorns, and Ascended Masters so that you can connect with the entire spiritual hierarchy. *Ask Your Angel Guides* takes you on a journey from creating a good relationship with your guardian angel to connecting with some of the beautiful, high-frequency spiritual energies that enhance your spiritual growth. I love this book and highly recommend it."

—**DIANA COOPER**, author of
The Golden Future and *The Wonder of Unicorns*
and founder of the Diana Cooper School of White Light

"In *Ask Your Angel Guides* Susan Browne has created a wonderfully transformative guide for anyone seeking to deepen their connection with angelic guides and to live a fulfilled and empowered life. This beautiful and insightful book offers profound wisdom and heartfelt encouragement for everyday spiritual growth. Her practical approach and deep spiritual insights empower the reader to ask for guidance, trust their intuition, and invite more clarity, well-being, and peace into their lives. This book is a must-read for anyone seeking to explore the loving support available from the angelic realms."

—**TONY ÆRCYUS CHRISTIE**, creator of
Melchizedek Labyrinth Healing and
author of *Labyrinth* and the *Labyrinth Wisdom Cards*

"Susan Browne offers a compassionate and powerfully practical guide for anyone seeking to deepen their spiritual connection. *Ask Your Angel Guides* is not only full of heart-centered wisdom—it's a true vibrational elevator. With grounded exercises, gentle insight, and joyful encouragement, Susan invites readers to co-create with the angelic realm and live with greater clarity, abundance, and peace. A beautiful read for modern spiritual seekers ready to open to divine guidance."

—**SANDRA RAE**, author of *Presence* and *Angels Aid* and host of the *Fiercely Spiritual* podcast

"Susan Browne offers a gentle yet powerful guide to connecting with our Angels. Her writing is infused with warmth, clarity, and a deep spiritual wisdom that invites us to open our hearts and trust in the loving presence of our Angels. In this book, Susan gives us the gift of accessing the Angelic energy and support always available to us. *Ask Your Angel Guides* is a beautiful guide for anyone on a journey of hope, healing, and Angelic connection. I am blessed to call Susan my friend and have been learning from her for many years—and will for many more to come."

—**CATHY HEALY**, Ballybunion yoga instructor

"Susan Browne's *Ask Your Angel Guides* is a fountain of love, wisdom, and light. In this book, you'll discover creative solutions to any issue or challenge you may encounter on your path. In a powerful way, it brings into your awareness that angels are by your side 24 hours a day, 7 days a week—lovingly waiting for you to ask for help and open to their blessings. Get your copy now—it will change your life."

—**FRANZISKA SIRAGUSA**, principal teacher with the Diana Cooper School of White Light and author of *Feng Shui with Archangels, Unicorns, and Dragons*

ASK *your* ANGEL GUIDES

How to Work with Celestial Energies to Create Abundance and Well-Being

SUSAN BROWNE

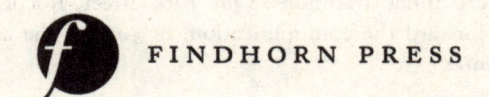

FINDHORN PRESS

Findhorn Press
One Park Street
Rochester, Vermont 05767
www.findhornpress.com

Findhorn Press is a division of Inner Traditions International

---

Disclaimer

The information in this book is given in good faith and is neither intended to diagnose any physical or mental condition nor to serve as a substitute for informed medical advice or care. Please contact your health professional for medical advice and treatment. Neither author nor publisher can be held liable by any person for any loss or damage whatsoever which may arise from the use of this book or any of the information therein.

Cataloging-in-Publication data for this title is available from the Library of Congress

ISBN 979-8-88850-350-8 (print)
ISBN 979-8-88850-351-5 (ebook)

Printed and bound in the United States by Lake Book Manufacturing, LLC

10 9 8 7 6 5 4 3 2 1

Edited by Jacqui Lewis
Illustrations by Susan Browne
Text design and layout by Richard Crookes
This book was typeset in Adobe Garamond Pro and Helvetica

To send correspondence to the author of this book, mail a first-class letter to the author c/o Inner Traditions, One Park Street, Rochester, VT 05767, USA and we will forward the communication, or contact the author directly at **https://angeleft.com**.

To Dad, with lots of love.

You are surrounded by angels.

Contents

Foreword

In our fast-paced world, moments of quiet connection to something greater can feel rare. Yet, in this book, Susan gently guides us into the warmth and peace of angelic presence, helping us reconnect with the love, protection, and wisdom that surround us every day. With each page, she invites us to look beyond the physical world and into the realm of angels, who are always near, waiting to offer their support.

One of the many gifts Susan brings to this work is her fresh and original perspective. Her approach to connecting with angels is uniquely heartfelt, making the practice feel accessible and relevant for today's world. Her insights are not only deeply spiritual but also practical and encouraging, showing readers that calling on angels can be a natural and joyful part of daily life.

Susan has a remarkable gift, one that transcends the words on the page. Her loving energy shines through each sentence, and you can almost hear her joyful, compassionate voice encouraging you as you read. Her guidance is filled with tenderness, making the path toward angelic connection feel welcoming and accessible. This book is not just a guide; it's a companion on the journey to deeper spiritual awareness and inner peace.

I have always felt that Susan herself is like an angel among us, sent here to share her gifts of kindness, healing, and love. Her presence is a blessing, and her words resonate with the same energy she brings to her personal interactions—a sense of deep caring and unwavering support. Reading *Ask Your Angel Guides*, you'll feel as if Susan is right beside you, walking with you through each chapter, encouraging you to reach out, to believe, and to trust in the angels' guidance.

This book is not only about calling on angels but about opening our hearts to the love that is always available to us, especially in times of need.

It's a book for anyone seeking comfort, reassurance, or a renewed sense of hope. Susan has created this work with great love, making it a treasure for all who wish to deepen their spiritual connection.

With gratitude and admiration, I recommend *Ask Your Angel Guides* to anyone ready to embrace the divine support that awaits us all. May it bring you the same sense of peace and joy it has brought to me.

With love and blessings,

—Meghaa Gupta, creator of the Cosmic Tree Foundation

Introduction

I hope that you will, if you don't already, ask the angels. A lot. For the small things as well as the big things. The angels want to help us with anything; they're never too busy, and they love to be asked.

In this book, I'm going to share some of the answers I have received when I asked the angels, and yet really the aim is for you to receive your own answers. Sometimes I will share a question with you so that you can ask it of the angels if it resonates. Other times I will also share the answer that came to me, either for myself or generally.

I've covered a range of topics, inspired by questions I ask myself, and common issues that arise for the many people I've had the pleasure of working with. Each topic is explored quite briefly, with the intention that those topics important to you are the ones you will dive more deeply into. Keep asking more questions to get more clarity.

When I refer to extra supports and information outside of this book, such as links, many of these are conveniently located for you on a page on my website: **https://angeleft.com/resources**.

Set an Intention Now

Intention is a powerful tool to use in life. Imagine it as a diamond finger of light you can project into the universe—be clear and precise for the greatest impact. Intention is always about what you *want*, and never about what you *don't want*.

If you've been to any of my talks or workshops you might know that I like participants to set an intention at the beginning. To ask the question: *what do I want from this?* Do this now, for this book.

Ask yourself: **what would I like to receive from this book?** Write your answer down.

Getting Started

I suggest starting out with questions that are not too cryptic to practise improving your confidence. For example, instead of something you've been agonizing over for a long time, try, *Angels, what clothes should I wear today to feel good?* Something more complex might invite mind chatter and you may feel as though it's not working. As you get better at it, you will know when you are connected to the angels.

My angels told me when I was about to start this book that I channel the answers more easily when I am writing with a pen as opposed to typing on a keyboard. That day I bought a new special notebook to help me create this book. I was bursting with joy at the counter, beaming from ear to ear, thinking about all the questions I might like to ask.

What Are Angels?

Angels are beings of light that work on a very high frequency, and this makes it hard for humans to perceive them. When you learn to tune in to angels—or even just open yourself to the possibility—they come closer to you. They are ready to work with you and are happy to guide you. They appear in most religions in one form or another, and in New Age spirituality, but the angels aren't exclusive to any one religion, nor does a person need to be religious to work with them. All that's needed is curiosity: I wonder if angels really exist? I asked myself that question.

My Angel Story

In 2005, a friend gave me a book about angels and I tried to read it, but it didn't quite resonate. I wasn't ready back then. These "angels" seemed too much like wishful thinking and a bit fluffy for me. A year later I couldn't have felt more differently. I developed an affinity for angel books, angel cards, and angel workshops which seemed to present themselves to me. It was as though they were looking for me, too.

I sought out knowledge about the chakras—the energy centres in and around the body—which was hugely helpful. I began to understand them as a sort of energy map to my life on all levels. Through visualization and calling in angels, practising yoga, and using colour and foods, I discovered ways to improve the areas in my life that needed attention at the time.

On two occasions I felt huge hands of light touching my back; I began to receive messages and know things without really understanding why or how. I started to see people's guardian angels at this time. The angels connected with me through humour and showed me things that made me laugh. They explained that they did this to lighten me up so I could see.

I don't go around seeing angels all the time. This might be nice but would be very distracting. To stay grounded and part of the world I've incarnated into, I usually just see angels when I ask to see them. Often in a meditative state or sometimes in my work.

Some people ask me, "What is my angel like?" I can only tell them how their angel presents to me specifically. When you see them yourself, they will appear perfectly for you with the message they want to convey. If you don't see them yet and want to, stay open.

Ask the question, *how can I help myself to see my angels?*

In 2009, I trained with the Diana Cooper Foundation (now the Diana Cooper School of White Light) and my experiences became yet richer. So much of what I know about angels is owing to the prolific work of Diana Cooper and the wonderful school she created and its teachers.

I never thought I would stand up in front of others and talk about angels but that is exactly what I began to do in the autumn of 2009, and I really enjoyed it. The energy people receive when they open up to the angelic realms is a delight to witness.

How to Address the Angels

The angels don't mind how you address them once your intention is clear. I like to say, "Angels . . . " or "Dear angels . . . ," then phrase my question. You can call upon specific angels, like an archangel, or the angels of Lemuria, or peace, for example, or the name of your guardian angel.

Don't worry about asking the "wrong" archangel if you don't yet know the qualities of each one. For example, you can ask Archangel Michael to help you with your writing project even though Archangel Gabriel is usually associated with writers. Or ask Archangel Gabriel to protect you, even though Archangel Michael is known for being an angel of great protection.

I think it's good to address the angels with confidence and kindness, as that just seems to work better in the world in general. Ask with a sense of expectation, like you respectfully anticipate the help being given. Yelling at angels or complaining to them isn't so useful—this is because angels are on a very high frequency and can't perceive all of our human denseness. Similarly, if we get into victim mode when we ask angels, they are less likely to be able to communicate with us effectively. Raise your frequency as high as you can to address them, and the communication will work better both ways.

On two occasions, though, I beseeched the angels when I was feeling hopeless, and they did help me. So, it's not that they won't help you unless you're in a high vibration, just that it's easier for both parties when you are.

Remember too that the angels are not meant to get us out of every fix we find ourselves in. There are some challenges we need for our soul growth; but the angels can help us to learn the lesson more quickly so we can assimilate it and move on. Some souls incarnate here on Earth with huge challenges to face. The angels won't take those challenges away but, if you ask, they will assist in getting through them and learning the incredible soul lessons that those challenges are meant to provide.

If you are already connected with your guardian angel, maybe you have a sense of what their name is. Some of you may have spirit guides that also feel like angels, such as deceased loved ones whose presence you perceive. This is different from your guardian angel even though they may well feel like an angel and have an angelic presence.

Questions as a New Superpower

When I became a life coach I learned about powerful questions and it helped me immensely, both in my Angel EFT and coaching practice and for myself. It was as though a(nother) light had been switched on. Our language and the words we use are very important and guide our life's course. Ask a question and you invite an answer, whether you ask yourself, another person, an angel, or thin air. Conversely, if you have a problem and you just keep thinking about how bad it is, the thoughts become cyclical and helpless.

Change the Energy

Try saying these two sentences out loud, allowing a pause in between:

I am so fed up with this problem.

How might I help myself to overcome this problem?

Note how they feel different. Once the problem is transformed into a question, we sense a totally new energy and power.

Some More Examples of Powerful Questions

How might I overcome this obstacle?

What else might help?

What have I learned about this that will inform the choice I make?

How could I reframe this issue as a goal?

What might success look like?

What do I want to see happen?

So to bring in the angels to make this even more powerful and get the support that is there for you, try rephrasing any current challenge to direct a question to the angels. For example,

Angels, how might I overcome this obstacle?

Channelling an Answer

When you pose a powerful question to yourself, immediately the mind gets busy reaching for an answer. To invite angelic answers:

- Use a piece of paper and pen if this resonates.

- Take some calming breaths and relax.

- Imagine you're becoming hollow so that light and angelic wisdom can flow through you.

- Ask your question and allow the answer to flow into you. Write down what comes through.

Don't agonize over if it's the angels or your mind that gives you the thought or answer. They can actually work together. You can also ask the questions in your mind and not use pen and paper, but it's great to start there as you are getting used to asking questions and receiving answers.

Ask Questions Every Day with an Angel Journal

My wish is for you to ask the angels something every day. Buy yourself a notepad, a simple one like kids use in school, if you like, or a pretty one. Get up a little earlier than usual so you can make space for this before your day starts, and write a question to help you with your day.

If you can't think of a question, simply write something like, *Angels, what do I need to know today?* Then relax and let yourself flow into an answer. You may feel as though you are simply answering yourself. And maybe you are. And if you are, you may well find that it comes from a wise, calm part of you, so it is good information anyhow. Be open. The more you use the word "angel" in your life, the more angels will come to you, and the easier it will get. Just like when you begin learning any new skill, at first it's hard and you're not sure you can do it. Then after a time, it's easy. You enjoy it and your confidence increases.

Not Just Angels

Next to angels and archangels, there are other high-frequency helpers that can help transform your life in amazing ways. They include:

- Unicorns

- Dragons

- Ascended Masters

- Nature spirits

When Diana Cooper told us she was going to lead a visualization to connect the group with unicorns in Dublin in 2009, at first I was skeptical. I thought, *really? Unicorns?* But I was blown away by the power of this visualization and the beautiful energy of the unicorns. I am open to the high-frequency spirit world now and realize that there are many high-vibrational helpers. In a forest, for example, all sorts of beautiful and unique spirits can present themselves.

But How Do I Know That It's Safe?

Some people worry that if they open themselves up to the spiritual realms they may also open themselves to less helpful entities or spirits. In this book I am going to share with you some ways of looking after your energy. But generally when your intention goes out to the angels, unless you are also asking (and therefore giving permission to) lower entities, you will attract only the angels and high-frequency spirit guides. If you still feel worried and want something immediately, then use this:

> *Archangel Michael, please protect me and all of my energy*
> *bodies now by placing me in your deep blue light. Thank you.*
> *It is done.*

Archangel Michael, a great warrior of light, is the energetic "bouncer" who keeps out all of the undesirables. You only need to ask, and he is there. Wear his deep blue light as a cloak, or a ball of light that acts as a layer at the outer edge of your aura, or use it like a shield. I like to imagine a great pyramid of blue light coming down over me. Then another, inverted pyramid comes up from below. The two merge and I am held within Archangel Michael's deep blue *merkabah* of light.

Here is another one to use if you feel you have absorbed someone else's negative stuff or let something less than light into your energy:

Archangels Zadkiel, Amethyst, and Gabriel, please activate the
Lilac Fire of Source in my energy fields now. Let it scan and
burn away and transmute anything less than light now.
And so it is.

The Lilac Fire of Source is also charged with love from the cosmic heart. It will transmute everything with kindness and grace. There are many such flames and fires and affirmations you can use. Find the ones that resonate the most and become familiar with them so they are easy for you to use.

How to Use This Book

I recommend to read this book from start to finish. However, some readers may want to jump ahead to chapters that speak to you because you have burning questions that you want to get to right away. And that's fine too.

Vibrational Elevators

I have read books that I consider *vibrational elevators*. Just reading them, even a page, has raised my vibration because of the energy and intention infused into the book that spills out to the reader. My hope is that reading this book acts as a vibrational elevator for you, moving you up the scale if you're not already at 10. Read about the scale in the following chapter.

PART ONE

THE ESSENTIALS

1

Vibration Affects Everything

The higher your vibration, the easier it is for you to perceive the messages your angels have for you. This is because the angels are on a high frequency, much higher than us. When we are operating in our higher vibrational states we can hear, feel, see, and sense so much easier. So before we start asking those questions, let's get clear on the vibrational scale. This is a tool you can come back to again and again to help you to maintain a high frequency and live a life that makes you delight in getting out of bed each morning.

To the left you see a vibrational scale I developed; the original is in color and you can download it from my website: **https://angeleft.com/resources**. Print out this vibrational scale or else draw your own if you like. Make it your bookmark; stick it on the fridge, or the bathroom mirror. Somewhere you'll see it a lot.

The vibrational scale is a subjective rating scale. It works for mood just as well as it works for vibrational frequency, but that's because they're almost always the same. The exceptions are with mood disorders that involve mania, and drug-induced highs, which are fear-based and therefore lower on the scale.

Fig.1: Vibrational Scale

Your Vibration Is NOT Fixed

A lot like the tide goes in and out, most of us go up and down the scale throughout our lives, our week, our day, and even our hour. This is because we're responding to life and the external, and also the internal. How we feel is shaped, too, by our hormones, neurotransmitters, gut health, nutrient levels, and the mind–body connection. No matter the basis, though, when our vibration is low we have the power to move it up higher. Today and even right now. We can help ourselves to experience and anchor those higher vibrational states so that they become our norm and the ones we *mostly* find ourselves in.

Becoming a Master of Your Vibration

Vibrational mastery is not about being at 10 all the time, but it means that your baseline, your typical vibration, is at the higher end. While we are in a human body, our vibration will not be static, and we respond to what's going on around us. Mastery means that you can quickly move back up if you slip down, but it's also about having compassion for the shadow aspect, which gravitates towards the lower end of the scale. More about this in Chapter 10.

Angels and Your Vibration

Angels function at a very high frequency, which is why most humans can't see them. As we raise our frequency, this becomes possible. When you deliberately connect with angels, they rush to meet you. It's as though they've been waiting in the wings for you to call them, which they have and are.

The word angel in all of its translations is a very high-frequency word. Just saying angel and nothing else can help to raise you up.

The angels like to give us signs to affirm their presence. These signs can vary from a very uplifting thought or insight to seeing angels, hearing them, or incredible synchronicities.

The Vibration of Our Questions

The higher the vibration of our question, the easier it is to manifest. For example, if we ask, *"Angels, how can I stop feeling so annoyed?"* this is a lower-vibrational question. Think of the opposite of annoyed and reach higher:

> *Angels, how can I feel more peaceful? How can I create the most amazing day today? How can I invite miracles and golden opportunities?*

This gets easier with practice. Write out questions that you like asking and have them to hand. These are especially useful for tougher moments when it's harder to stretch for those higher-vibrational questions.

Vibration Across Life Aspects

You can measure how you are feeling right now and this number will give you an overall picture of your vibrational frequency. Then, if it's not 10 already, ask the question,

> *Angels, what's one thing I can do right now to help myself move up one place?*

You can also rate the different areas of your life. Quite often they are similar. It's not common, for example, for someone to have a partner relationship score of 1 and to be an overall 10—the low vibration of the partner relationship score will pull down the overall score. Similarly if the person's life is going great on all levels except an unhealthy diet, or they have an addiction that pulls their energy. We can ignore and turn a blind eye to those problems for a time, depending on what's going on in our lives, but generally it depletes our vibration.

It may be useful to look at those lower areas of life to help pull up your overall vibration. And seek help for difficult areas, so that you can master the lessons and not have to keep experiencing those lower numbers. Only you know what is most useful to focus on now. Do remember to come back to things that give you the most joy. Life is for enjoying, as well as for the learning that we all came here for. And the more joy you can see, the easier it will be to live in the higher-frequency bands.

What Lights You Up?

Recently I visited one of my favourite places—the UK town of Glastonbury. I've been visiting Glastonbury since childhood and, even though it was far away, I'm lucky to have a mum who always loved it there too, and still does. I used to save up pocket money so I could buy crystals when we visited. I didn't know anywhere else that sold them at that time, and I always adored them. I haven't changed all that much. I still like to buy a crystal from Glastonbury, and I ask that it is infused with that very special energy that flows there.

I climbed St Michael's Tor for sunrise—food for the soul. But the night before, I didn't sleep much. I could feel an enormous crystal, possibly an etheric one, under the Tor and under Glastonbury. It seemed to glow and pulsate, and I understood why I love it there so much. I've known for a while that there is a network of leylines under Glastonbury and the enormous crystal makes perfect sense.

I walked the labyrinth in the town centre, to release all that stuff I no longer wanted to carry, and focused on what I wanted to bring in. What I'm creating in my life. I am sharing this story with you because I invite you to think now of:

- Places that you love.

- Things that you love.

- Activities that you love.

- What lights you up?

- What do you love to do?

Putting pictures of the things and places you love around you and on your devices as screensavers can help raise your vibration. Also, we will look at vision boards in more detail later, but for now I'll say that when you create a vision board, remember to put photos of lovely memories on it as well as the things you wish to manifest, as this increases your joy and gratitude for what you have already received.

My intention in writing this book is to help as many people as possible to live in joy and to feel the magic of life. Because the more people are living in a high-vibrational state the better the world becomes.

We All Rise Together

Competition and one-upmanship are lower-dimensional mindsets. What you wish for yourself, wish also for others. The idea that there isn't enough to go around is a myth. We can all rise together. This is how oneness works. Oneness sits in your navel chakra at the fifth-dimensional frequency.

Place your hands there now and breathe that in. "We are all one. We are all connected. What I wish for myself I wish for everyone. Happiness, joy, peace, bliss, abundance, confidence, laughter, love, connection, and all good things."

A lovely exercise to do that strengthens oneness consciousness is to see, in your mind's eye, strangers receiving blessings. As you pass people on the street, have the thought, "Blessings of love and joy to you," or "Blessings of abundance coming your way today." This is very uplifting, and, as if that weren't enough, what you wish for others has a tendency to also come to you.

It's Easier to Do Things
When Our Frequency Is High

I have noticed that when my vibration is high, I can get things done in less time and expend less energy. Like I am being carried by some sort of golden light stream that flows through my hands and body. As though it's not just me doing it, but I've got help. My understanding of this is that, being in a high vibration, I open myself to the assistance of the light beings around me. To more light. I have felt that while writing this book; at times, it has practically written itself. Most writers, without realizing, act as channels, putting themselves out as a vessel for ideas to flow through. The angels tell me that is how this book has been so easy to write—because I have been working within this light stream.

The food we eat has a frequency, and when we overeat, which is so common and encouraged in Western society, we feel slowed down and sluggish. Instead of seeking outside things like food to "fill us up," we can learn to fill ourselves up with light and gratitude. And we will then naturally reach for lighter foods that are in alignment with our frequency.

Imagine yourself, if you aren't already, at 10 on the scale. How might you walk differently, and talk differently? What might your day look like? Try to imagine yourself, for now, in your current life and location, rather than conjuring up images of yourself in far-flung places or with a very different lifestyle. As the saying goes, "wherever you go, there you are." So imagine yourself at 10 just where you are now. In this body, these clothes, this place, this situation.

If we place conditions on our happiness (I'll feel great when . . .) then we move the higher ends of the scale out of reach. More about this later.

Thoughts and Focus Are Everything

Our thoughts and the things we say influence our experience. There are many spiritual laws, and the law of attraction—which says we create everything with our thoughts—is just one of them. So it's important to remember that, when something happens, it's not always the case that you attracted it with your thoughts. That is one possibility, but there are others—our ancestral lineage and family patterns, and our soul's journey, to name just two. The law of attraction is hugely useful though in reminding us of the things we can influence. **If our thoughts are creating our reality, with or without other influences, then cleaning up our thoughts has to be a good idea.**

Archangel Jophiel helps us with raising our thoughts. Try asking:

Archangel Jophiel, what can I do to raise my thoughts
right now?

Throughout this book, I will come back to this point about thoughts and encourage you to become an avid listener to your thoughts and your language. To do this creates mastery. To become a master of your thoughts is to unlock the vastness of your potential.

I often ask the angels:

Angels, how can I help raise my vibration today?

Answers I typically receive are things like this:

- Make a list of things you want to get done today so you can focus

- Exercise

- Do that thing you've been putting off so that it stops pulling your energy

- Get out in nature

- Have a break from your phone

- Eat wisely

- Drink water

- Angel EFT tapping

- Connect with a friend

- Make a gratitude list

- Listen to an uplifting audiobook

- Clean something

- Come back to your goals and intention

- Meditate

- Spend 25 minutes decluttering

- Swim (wild swimming is best of all but pools are also good)

- Practise *pranayama* (yogic breathing), mindful breathing, or any breathing technique you are familiar with that you like

- Engage your sense of smell with some aromatherapy oils or a room spray

What answers did you get? Write them down.

2

Angels and Other Helpers

This book is called *Ask Your Angel Guides*, but I ask other helpers too that I also want to share with you. In this chapter, I'm going to summarize the angels and also some of the other helpers that I consider to be in the angelic realms or heavenly helpers. Benevolent, generous light beings who are committed to assisting us and our world to realize our exquisite full potential.

Angels

Angels are known as messengers of God and appear in all of the main religions we have in the world, but with different names. Even if we never acknowledge it, we each have one guardian angel who is with us from before we are born and who stays with us our whole life. Perhaps many other angels too. Your guardian angel wants the best for you, and for you to fulfil your mission.

We came to Earth with a mission and after we were born we went through the veils of amnesia whereby we forgot what we came here for. Earth is a very dense plane compared to where we came from beforehand, so it's no surprise. Many souls ask to come here because of the huge learning opportunities. Our job in this life is to remember and fulfil our mission. Many people who identify with being lightworkers say that their mission is simply to bring more light. When they fine-tune this, they see that they have many gifts and talents and things that really light them up. Some have one core gift that they will use over all others, and other people have many and use them at different times. When we find our gifts we can truly shine.

The archangels are overlighting angels and are, just like Source or God, omnipresent.

One of the biggest challenges for humans learning to connect with angels is the worry that they are somehow bothering or burdening the angels or archangels by asking for help. This couldn't be further from the truth. The angels are waiting to work with you and guide you. Ask every day throughout the day. Ask for everything and anything. Imagine having your own guide who champions you and wants to help you by your side always. This is what you have. Ask. Then be open to the signs and guidance.

Mildred, who worked with me, explained that she was feeling overwhelmed with bills but was reluctant to ask the angels for help with finances. Her understanding was that, if you were to pray, it must be for something very important or virtuous, and never for material gain, because the angels would disapprove. In fact, the angels love to help us to pay our bills and open ourselves to prosperity. When we are relaxed and happy (rather than stressed because we don't have enough money), we are more likely to be of service to others. If you like, think of it as a two-way exchange. Angels sometimes work through humans to help humanity. Have you ever had the experience of another person acting like an angel to you? Helping you out when you were in dire need? Saving you from something? Acting as a guiding light? It is true that angels can step into us and work through us. When we are taking care of ourselves, are comfortable and our needs are met, our energy is typically more pure and bright, and we are better channels for the angels.

This doesn't mean that people experiencing poverty cannot serve and do the angels' work. We know from certain religious orders that this isn't the case, like the Poor Clares, which St Clare of Assisi founded in 1212. But you do not need to be poor to advance on your spiritual path.

If you are still on the fence about whether or not angels can really exist, then imagine that your angel is in fact a part of you that wants what is best for you. Like your higher self, or your greatest, most evolved self. You might call it your "angel self." In a way this is true, since while angels are not human, if we are all one and all connected to Source then our angels are, in a sense, like an aspect of us.

How to Receive Angel Guidance

First of all, be open to the possibility. If you open your mind to realize that there might be angels trying to help you and guide you, this makes you more receptive to signs, and to accepting them with an open heart. Today, we prize science and hard evidence. And for many things this is helpful. But when it comes to angel signs and guidance, you need to use another part of your brain. Allow yourself to relax your mind into delightful awe, or childlike wonder. This doesn't mean losing control, or being foolish. It means coming to trust that there is an invisible world that we cannot yet capture through our scientific lens but that, when we open ourselves up to it, will change our lives in miraculous ways.

Not Wanting to Hear

Sometimes when we start to engage with the spiritual realms, we worry about hearing the messages in case we don't like what they're telling us. The mind might chatter on, saying things like, *I don't want to hear what they want to tell me. I already know these things are not in alignment, and I don't need them to tell me about this.* And so on.

Remember, the angelic realms are not a panel of judges waiting to criticize us or cast their vote on how we are doing. They are loving guides who know that being human can be hard.

Your Angel's Messages

People often ask, how can I tell if a "message" is a thought in my head or the angels? I know by the way it feels. If I receive angel guidance I recognize its high frequency; it is beautiful, reassuring, loving, compassionate, and makes me feel good. The angels don't tell us scary things, although they may warn us with a strong feeling to avoid something or make a different choice.

If our minds do this same thing, giving us high-frequency messages that feel angelic, then this is because we have raised our frequency to tune in to the angels and so can think in this way.

Once, during meditation, the angels foretold me about a dangerous situation coming up in my day. My soul sometimes yearns for adventure and excitement and that day I was going sea swimming. I noted the message, and my friend and I were warned by other swimmers, but we went swimming in that place anyway. Sure enough, as the tide turned we began to wade back to the beach, skirting the edges of the sea caves, but the currents strengthened around us, stopping us from going any further. We were forced to go back through the caves and climb the rough, slippery way back onto the cliff path. It was an important lesson in sea safety as well as in heeding angelic warnings.

Once we had got out of the water, I looked at my phone, which I had with me in a plastic pouch. All by itself, the screen unlocked and opened up an Archangel Michael angel card app I use. It self-selected the card "Courage" for me. Archangel Michael told me he was with us and, along with our guardian angels, had got us out of the current.

We have free will and can choose dangerous actions. The angels can't step in unless Source directs them to intervene.

Unicorns

Unicorns are great beings of spiritual light who help us to manifest our soul's desires. In recent years, unicorns have come into the collective consciousness because they are helping humans now in a big way and we are ready to work with them again for the first time since Golden Atlantis. You can connect with your own personal unicorn, ask them their name, and call upon them just like you do an angel. Their energy is very joyful and light and they exude love, helping us to feel peace, hope, delight, magic, and mystery. Although they are brilliant white, I also see crystal, silver, gold, and rainbow colours around the unicorns.

You can send the unicorns out ahead of you at the start of your day, then notice how your day goes. Imagine them spinning silver light out ahead of you, smoothing the way for good opportunities, or healing or easing, whatever it is you are looking for today. The more open and relaxed you are, the stronger your connection will be.

Connect with Your Unicorn

1. Ask your unicorn to connect with you now, close your eyes, and allow yourself to feel their energy.

2. Your unicorn directs its golden horn of light towards the centre of your forehead, and this helps to clear and open your third eye so that you can see.

3. Relax and notice the sensations as your unicorn makes their presence known to you.

4. Ask them their name.

5. Look into their eyes.

6. Ask how you might work together.

Rowan Trees as Guardians

Rowan trees are protective and are connected to the unicorns. Soon after I learned this, I was given a rowan tree and I planted it in my garden. Perhaps you will notice these trees now if they grow where you live.

Connect with a Rowan Tree

1. Stand near a rowan tree and ask to connect with it. If you cannot do so physically, look up a picture of a rowan tree or imagine one. Imagine making a heart connection with the tree.

2. Now see the tree pulsating with shimmering white and silver lights, and unicorns gathering around it and around you.

3. Breathe in this beautiful light. Imagine it filling up your aura. You are deeply protected and loved.

Dragons

Dragons are great loving beings who can access lower dimensions more easily than angels. In some cultures, my own included, we learn about dragons being scary, usually as monsters that threaten people and terrorize communities. Yet in Chinese culture the dragon is revered and is a good luck symbol. You can call upon the dragons just as you can the angels. If you want more courage, say simply: *Dragons, please help me with this.* I highly recommend Diana Cooper's book *Dragons, Your Celestial Guardians* for gaining a deeper understanding.

Dragons Help Us with World News

When watching the news or if you hear about something disturbing, asking the dragons to help is one thing you can do. Close your eyes and say, "*Dragons, please go to* [insert name of the place/situation]."

When we worry, we add to a collective cloud of fear that only makes things worse, so always ask. In my blog "Send Angels to Someone Else," you will find tips that also apply to dragons or any angelic beings.

You can send dragons into murky, heavy areas that the angels cannot access because of their high frequency; the dragons will help to clear energies and raise things up. Each of the dragons are associated with one of the elements—earth, fire, water, and air. Earth dragons work in the earth, although they also breathe fire. They help to clear the leylines and to ground you. Fire dragons are masters at clearing energies and protecting you. Water dragons will help you to move around obstacles in life, and to "be in the flow." Air dragons help us to raise our thoughts. There are many different types of dragon and some have more than one, even three, elements. One example, which we will look at later, is the rainbow dragons. The dragons also work on different dimensions, depending on their purpose.

You can have a dragon who is assigned to work with you just like a guardian angel, although it's not quite the same as you usually only have a dragon at your side if you choose to work with them. Call forth your personal dragon. Notice what element they are, what colours they have, how big or small they are. Ask them their name and, if you don't receive it right away, be patient and open to receiving it later; then write it down and remember it. Make the connection stronger by calling on your dragon for help and guidance, just like you might with your angel.

Types of Dragon

Earth Dragons

David was passionate about creating a space in his community for growing organic vegetables. There was a site earmarked for this project and there was funding and support to go ahead. But things kept getting in the way and he couldn't get started. David got so frustrated, he felt like giving up. But together we did a remote clearing on the land with the earth dragons. He saw clairvoyantly that there was historic karma connected to the area, and the dragons were able to clear it. A week later, David received a phone call to say that he could go ahead and start making the raised beds. He could hardly believe it. Everything flowed beautifully after that.

Earth dragons look after the earth and the soil, the crystals and minerals. They can clear the leylines of the planet.

One day I was going on a journey and I picked the earth dragon card from Diana Cooper's dragon cards. I asked for more information and I was told that I was being assigned the task of bringing healing to a particular place that had been in the news lately, concerning a scandal. I was to work with the earth dragons to clear the energy of where this occurred. I looked on the map and, sure enough, this place was on my route. The dragons told me I was to leave a rose quartz heart there, so I brought this with me.

When I arrived in the town, I didn't like to ask anyone where the place was. I felt sure the locals didn't want people from all ends of the country coming to have a look. There had been enough in the media about it already. I asked my guides to show me where to go. *Cross over*, came the strong thought and, sure enough, the entrance was across the street. I was able to add some healing and leave the crystal there.

In this case I had been given the assignment to visit physically, and felt glad to go there, but we can always work remotely to heal places. Ask the earth dragons to go to sites of war, hurt, and strife where you cannot go. Like the angels, the dragons like to be asked.

Water Dragons

Water dragons can raise the energy of the water you drink, and also the water in your body. You can call on them to purify the water in your body, to bring light to every cell, and to bless the rivers, the oceans, the rain, and all water. Where there are droughts or floods, ask the water dragons to help. They also help us to be in flow more, as water is the teacher of flow.

Air Dragons

Air dragons can raise our thoughts. Call them and Archangel Jophiel in to release and blow away unhelpful thoughts and to help you create new, high-vibrational thoughts. You can also call upon the air dragons during a storm to keep yourself safe or protect loved ones.

Storms and strong winds are nature's way of having a good clear-out. Walking in the wind can be very healing. When you do, ask the air dragons to purify you so that your experience goes even deeper.

Fire Dragons

Fire dragons are master purifiers. You can ask them to burn away things that aren't serving you, in your energy fields, in your physical space, in your chakras, and in your body. When we have a fever, the body is attempting to burn up the infection in its own resourceful way. Ask the fire dragons to create the heat needed to burn up things that you want to heal and release. If you suffer hot flashes or night sweats, ask the fire dragons to help guide you in understanding anything that you can influence that causes the body to fire up in this way. Often dietary changes can make a difference.

Have you ever photographed fire? It's quite magical. You might notice that in the photos you can see the shapes of dragons and salamanders.

If you've had an argument, ask the fire dragons to come and clear the space around you. Invite them to burn away any toxic exchanges between you and others, including individuals, groups, institutions, or even the fear within the collective consciousness. Ask them to bring more passion into your life, or to stoke up your enthusiasm for something or for life in general.

Ascended Masters

Many of the ascended masters, unlike angels, have lived as humans on Earth. Through those lifetimes, they underwent profound spiritual initiations, mastering lessons in love, wisdom, and service. These initiations elevated their vibrational frequency to the point of ascension—transitioning beyond the cycle of reincarnation and into higher spiritual realms, where they now serve as guides and teachers. Often referred to as masters of spiritual wisdom, some also appear as gods and goddesses in the religions that we know today.

The Rays

The Rays are an aspect of Source embodied for Earth. Initially seven, there are now thought to be many more. Each Ray has its own ascended master, also called the chohan, who carries the energy of that Ray.

The ascended masters appear in the religions that we know today. Here is a list of some ascended masters and some example questions that you may like to ask that may have relevance for you. Of course, just like the angels, you can ask any of the masters anything.

- **El Morya**—chohan of the first ray of power, will, and purpose. A question you might ask: *Dear El Morya, how can I stay authentic in my energy?* I have a blog on this topic.

- **Lord Gautama**—chohan of the tenth ray. Has the purity of the Buddha energy. *Lord Gautama, how do I create more space and discipline in my life for meditation?*

- **Hathor**—Egyptian great mother goddess and master of the sixth ray. *Dear Hathor, how can I feel more confident as a mother?*

- **Master Hilarion**—chohan of the fifth ray and helps scientists and spiritual leaders. *Dear Master Hilarion, how may I uncover the truth today?*

- **Jesus** (Sananda)—master of the second ray, works with the Gold Ray of Christ. *Master Jesus, how may I forgive myself today so that I might truly thrive?*

- **Krishna**—a cosmic master. By chanting *Om Sri Krishnah sharanam namah* we invite the removal of grief and misery from our minds so that we may feel peace.

- **Lord Kumeka**—lord of light and chohan of the eighth ray. *Dear Lord Kumeka, how may I fully remove negative energies from my being today so that I radiate the light of my full potential?*

- **Kuthumi**—Teacher and master of the second ray. *Dear Lord Kuthumi, how may I assist with the evolution of the planet?*

- **Quan Yin**—goddess of mercy and compassion. Chohan of the twelfth ray, of unconditional love. *Dearest Quan Yin, how may I have more compassion for this person/situation?*

- **Lord Lanto**—chohan of the second ray, the ray of love and wisdom. *Lord Lanto, how may I fully activate my illumined self today?*

- **Lady Mary Magdalene**—chohan of the sixth ray of idealism and devotion and brings the divine feminine into religion. *Dear Lady Mary Magdalene, how can I balance my masculine and feminine energies perfectly today?*

- **Lady Nada**—chohan of the seventh ray. *Dear Lady Nada, how may I offer comfort and healing to my inner child today?*

- **Paul the Venetian**—chohan of the third ray of intelligence and creativity. *Dear Master Paul the Venetian, what can I do towards my creative project today?* Or be more specific about your project. Ask him for inspiration or guidance, or discipline.

- **St Germain**—master and bringer of the violet flame, along with Archangel Zadkiel. *Dear St Germain, how may I work with the violet flame today to improve my life?*

- **Lord Rakoczy**—chohan of the eleventh ray of clarity, mysticism, and healing. Also known as the Great Director, Lord Rakoczy works with world leaders and is helping to raise the frequency of world religions to release old, unhelpful patterns. *Lord Rakoczy, how might I rise above third-dimensional thought forms today and access my divine wise self?*

- **Lord Voosloo**—chohan of the ninth ray of harmony. *Dear Lord Voosloo, how may I raise my thoughts and beliefs today?*

- **Serapis Bey**—chohan of the fourth ray of Harmony and Balance. Also carries the White Flame of Ascension. *Dear Serapis Bey, how can I help to heal my physical body now?*

Connect with Your Angelic Team

1. Bring to mind the things that you love. What makes your heart sing? Release heaviness and breathe in light.

2. Ask the angels and angelic beings that make up your team to step forward now so that you see who they are.

3. Are there unicorns? Dragons? Ascended masters? Other angelic beings? Allow them to form a circle around you and feel as they shine their combined light over you. Connect with each of them, eye to eye, heart to heart.

4. These are the guides that are currently helping you.

5. Thank each of them and bring yourself back into the room. Feel your feet on the floor. Drink water.

6. Make a note of your team so you remember them all.

Become a Master of Your Energy

In your journal or on a piece of paper, note down all the areas of your life you can think of. Some people like to use the wheel of life. You can download a blank one of these at: **https://angeleft.com/resources**, or simply draw your own into your journal. I've inserted a sample here. Note down each of the categories that matter to you right now. Go ahead and create your own categories or headings that matter most to you.

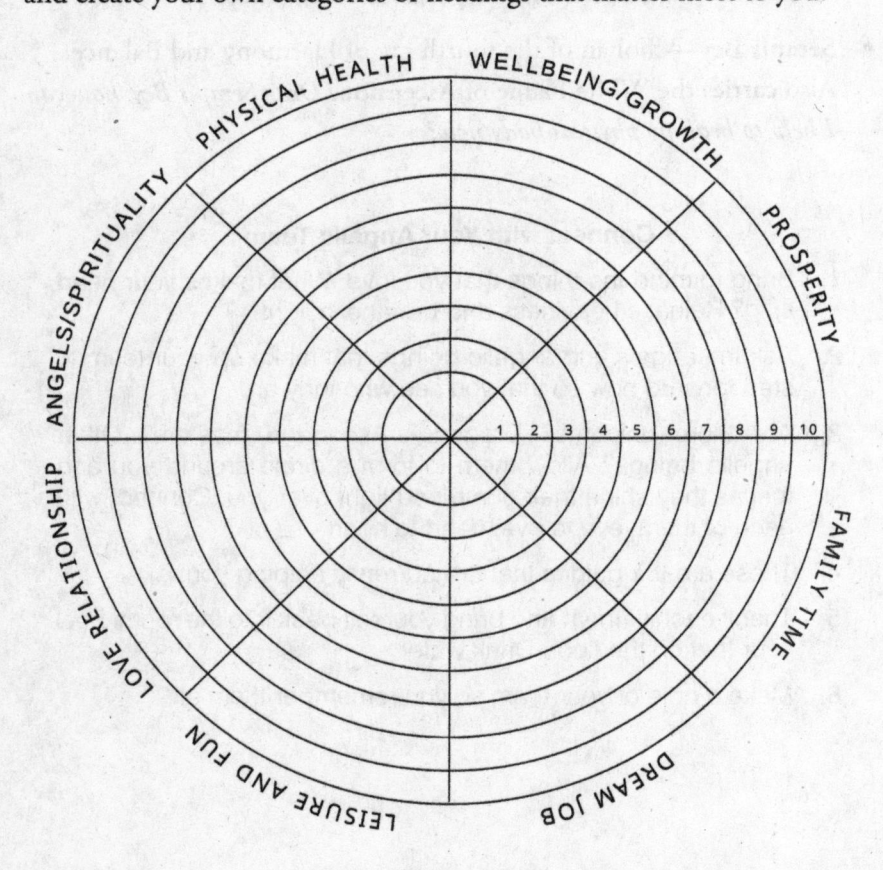

Fig.2: Wheel of Life

The chapter titles of this book might help to give you ideas if you need them. Now, using the vibrational scale on page 21, rate each category out of ten. When you're done you will have a nice map of what's doing well and where there's room for improvement. If there are a lot of categories at the lower end of the scale, these will pull down your overall vibration and ability to attract good things. The more expanded it looks, with higher numbers, the higher your overall vibration baseline is likely to be. You could even get fancy and colour it in according to the colours of the scale if you like.

Keep this somewhere you can come back to later, and, if you printed one off, print off another that you can fill again in 21 days or when you've finished this book.

Using the Wheel of Life to Decide What to Work on Today

It can be tempting to work on many things simultaneously, but try to focus on just one today. When you look at your wheel, what is asking for your attention today? Ask the angels, *What should I work on today?* Remember that, when we heal one area of our lives, it sometimes has this wonderful effect of also raising the vibration of other areas. This is because nothing exists truly in isolation, but is affected by the whole. You will know when it's time to move on to something else. And if you need to come back to something, that's fine too.

Raise Your Vibration Before You Begin

If you are feeling sad, angry, or any of the negative emotions common to the lower end of the scale, it's hard to make improvements. So if this is the case, ask:

> *Angels, how can I help myself to move one place up the scale right now?*

You don't need to be high up on the scale to do this work, as the work itself and reading this book is designed to bring your vibration up. Just know that, when you work on your vibration, everything gets easier. If you are at the lower end of the scale, make this a priority, so then everything else can improve. Go back to page 21 as many times as you need to check your vibration, or print out the scale so you can keep it to hand and refer to it easily.

Another similar question I ask is:

Angels, how can I feel better right now?

Bring to mind the things that you love. What makes your heart sing? Release heaviness and breathe in light. Your essence is as light as a feather. Let go of the illusions that the mind creates and move into your essence now.

The above is what the angels told me. Any time you're feeling low or just so-so, ask one of those questions. Does your mind go blank or does something pop into your head right away? If nothing comes at first, take a breath and ask it again. You are wise beyond belief and you have many of the answers to your questions inside you. The angels have the keys to help us unlock the answers that are already within.

Asking the Right Question

The angels reminded me again and again while writing this book to ask the right question. For example, if I asked, *How can I overcome this bad mood?*, they would advise me to try instead focusing on the opposite of a bad mood. So, you would ask yourself, what is the opposite of this mood? Is it joy? Freedom? Excitement? Energy? Make a list of all the things that might be the positive opposite of the bad mood. Then using these words create a new question that includes one of those. For example,

Angels, how do I feel more joy in my life?

Mind Manifesting Tip

When you are trying to get rid of anything negative, always seek out its opposite. Think of the other end of the scale. The mind hears the negative word and gets busy conjuring up the meaning and images associated with that. It doesn't hear "overcome," or "get rid of," so if you say, "I want to get rid of money worries," the mind makes a beeline for money worries. Instead, say, "I want prosperity," or "I want money confidence," and the mind will hear this and gravitate this way.

Connecting with the Magic and Playing Games

Children understand magic and we can learn a lot by watching them play. When I was a child I had some dolls called *Flower Fairies*. A best friend and I would play for hours with these fairies. We would leave them in places around the garden and then go inside for a while, to give them a chance to "move on their own." Of course, when we came back to the garden to find them they always had! My friend's mum may have played a part in this but I think, even if she hadn't physically moved those fairies, we were so in tune with magic that our eyes would have seen subtle movements that they had made.

I can still feel the bliss when I recall childhood memories such as this one. Adventures, reading books, writing stories, and make-believe all evoked this feeling of magic.

As adults, many of us have been primed to question everything and to think there's always a scientific and logical explanation. This started when we began school and maybe even before. Magic is only for kids, after all. But is it really?

I invite you to play games in your life to see if you can start feeling the magic again—if you're not already. Manifesting things is one way to get magic flowing. A few years ago I told a family member that I was going to find a lime-green jumper and it would cost €17.99. They looked at me like I was joking, and I just smiled. I had asked the angels to help, and I felt so certain. A little while later they met me coming from the checkout and gasped when I showed them the lime-green jumper with the price tag: €17.99. Usually, I wouldn't need to be as specific as this, it was just a game I wanted to play. But I think it demonstrates the idea nicely.

If you need to buy something today, try asking the "shopping angels" to help you to find what you want and any other specifics you would like. I am much more conscious since then about my shopping choices and caring for Earth, so would now specify: a good price, kind to the planet, and ethically produced. They can certainly help us in charity shops as well. Call the angels in your mind: *Angels, please help me to find the perfect . . . for . . .* , then let go.

Allow yourself to get excited about finding this ideal item, whatever it is. If it's clothes, see yourself putting them on and admiring how you look. When we buy second-hand, we're giving something a second chance. Ask Archangel Zadkiel to clear second-hand items of other people's energy and attune it to yours, so you can best work together. Do this with new things as well, and send thanks to all the people and planetary materials that helped make it.

Chakras and Vibration

When I learned about the 12 fifth-dimensional chakras with Diana Cooper some years ago, it brought my spiritual practice to a whole new level. At that time there were special physical exercises to activate those chakras, but now we can use visualization. With conscious awareness, you can release anything from any of your chakras that no longer serves, and rewrite old patterns. See more on how to activate and work with the chakras in my YouTube videos.

Here I provide a brief outline of the 12 chakras and what they are associated with. You will also find the name of the respective Archangel overseeing each chakra.

- **Earth Star Chakra** = Deep connection with Mother Earth and bringing spirit into matter. Archangel Sandalphon.

- **Base Chakra** = Grounding, fifth-dimensional knowing that all is looked after and you are provided for. Archangel Gabriel.

- **Sacral** = Creativity and sexuality. Healing the divine feminine and the divine masculine. Delight. Parenting. Archangel Gabriel.

- **Navel** = Oneness consciousness—the grid of light that connects us all. Archangel Gabriel.

- **Solar Plexus** = Blazing golden light of wisdom and confidence. Archangel Uriel.

- **Heart** = Deep love for one and all. Archangel Chamuel.

- **Throat** = Divine communication and expression. Archangel Michael.

- **Third Eye** = Divine manifestation. Archangel Raphael.

- **Crown** = Whole connection with the higher spiritual realms. Fifth-dimensional thoughts. Archangel Jophiel.

- **Causal** = Portal or entry point for many angels, unicorns, and other angelic beings and masters. Archangel Christiel.

- **Soul Star** = Access to Divine Energy and soul mission. Archangel Mariel.

- **Stellar Gateway** = Merging with the Monad, claircognizance (clear knowing). Being a beacon of light. Archangel Metatron.

The chakras cover every aspect of our life. All of our desires, facets, personality traits, physicality, dreams, and everything else is charted in our chakras, which can teach us so much if we tune in to them.

PART TWO

FABULOUS MANIFESTING WITH ANGELS

Prosperity and Money

Angels, how can I feel more prosperous?

Tidy your home. Let it be part of each day. Value what you have—let go of what you don't value. Heavy energies and memories lower the vibration. Let them go with love. Release clothes that are too small, too big, or that you don't enjoy wearing. Trust that beautiful clothes will come your way again. Believe in a beautiful flow. Know that all good things come to you with ease and grace.

Do you see that all-important word in the question above? The word "feel." How can I feel prosperous? How can I feel abundant? How can I feel good about money? Abundance and prosperity are a feeling. Someone can have millions and feel poor, and someone else can have very little and feel wealthy. Money tends to follow our feelings, so if we feel poor it tends not to go very far. We are tense and don't invite good money opportunities; things are expensive, or we make rash decisions and fritter away money. Conversely, for the person who has little but feels wealthy, they attract abundance in the form of things they need, money, and opportunity.

Angels, how can I heal my relationship with money?

Where are you on the vibrational scale when you say the word "money?" Or when you handle your bank card or cash? When you receive money? When someone asks you for money unexpectedly, or when a bill arrives? All of these are clues as to how you feel about money and where your vibration is. Say the affirmations below and note how true they feel to you, out of ten. If any of these are below seven then make a note of them and set your intention to work to bring that number up in order to heal your relationship with money.

- I am prosperous.
- I invite the easy flow of money.
- I embody abundance.
- I welcome income.
- I open the door to good things in my life.
- I say yes to wonderful opportunities.

Some years ago I posted a tapping video for manifesting a thousand euros. One viewer explained in the comments how she had tapped along to the video and then manifested the money to pay for the course of her dreams – a dog psychology course in LA.

Being Clear About Why You Want More Money

Why do you want more money than you have? Ask yourself this so that you are clear. It might be that you have debts you want to pay off. You want to buy a car. To be able to move. Or you'd like to pay off your mortgage so you don't owe anything. Or to have enough to just be able to pay the bills without stress.

Would you like to have a great big savings account as a rainy-day fund? Or for your future? For your loved ones? To help worthy causes? For adventures? To wear beautiful clothes that make you feel graceful? To have a beautiful garden? To plant a forest? The more clarity you have on the details, the better.

Worries About Wanting Money

Some people are afraid of asking God or the angels for money in case it's wrong. But whatever your beliefs, your beliefs matter, because your subconscious mind won't allow you to pretend otherwise. If you are held back by outdated beliefs that don't support you any more, take active steps to change these beliefs. You could ask: *Angels, how do I upgrade my beliefs to more supportive ones?*

The love of money itself can be harmful if it moves into the lower vibrations of ego, one-upmanship or trying to have power over another. If you find yourself thinking, *I want loads of money so that I can compete or best someone else,* or, *so I can drive a car that makes me feel superior to others,* this is fear-based. This lower-frequency desire to show off or use money as a tool of power or status is third-dimensional and the angels step back from it.

If you want money for yourself, want it for someone else too. In her beautiful book, *The Power*, Rhonda Byrne tells a story about how her sister manifested a new car because she cried tears of joy for a sibling when they got something they wanted. She goes on to say that, when you see something you want belonging to another, try to feel as joyful and excited as if you have that thing yourself. Open your heart to be thrilled for that other person, and it will open up the channels for you to attract it to yourself. This can be a hard lesson, especially if you've been telling yourself, *good fortune like that only happens to other people, never me.* But with intention, you'll change the narrative and start to feel different.

Affirm: *I am so glad that they have . . . and I feel so excited that it's coming to me too.*

Considerations When Playing the Lottery

I don't generally play the lottery or gamble, or at least very rarely. This is because I can feel the heavy collective energy of desperation and fantasy around it. It also reminds me of being a teen and winning the jackpot on a fruit machine, then being hooked on those machines for some months afterwards, until I learned the lesson. I had wasted far more money than I had won and decided this wasn't for me.

Many people play the lottery who have gambling addictions, but of course many others also play for fun or simply to facilitate another possibility of bringing in more money. If you can play the lottery or similar with an open heart and without underlying fantasy or desperation—in other words, if you feel authentic in your own energy when you play—then it is likely harmless.

If you want to win the lottery, I would suggest moving your focus to allowing in money, and a large sum of it, if this is what you truly want and feels in alignment. Money can come in so many ways, we can't possibly imagine them. If you play the lottery, how does it make you feel? If it makes you feel excited and joyous then this is a good vibration. Check in with excitement to make sure it is connected to joy and not fear masked by giddiness and unreality, which is typical of those with gambling issues. This is like a false high and is fear in disguise.

Research has shown time and again that those who win the lottery often lose it and end up owing lots. This happens when they successfully manifested the money but then didn't do the work to correct poverty consciousness. Through fear of losing the money they lost it.

Poverty Consciousness vs. Prosperity Consciousness

Look at the vibrational scale at the beginning of this book. You can apply it to poverty (0) versus prosperity consciousness (10). Where are you on the scale right now? We can go up and down the scale even in one day. What could you do today that will move you up one place, if you are not already at 10? People at 8 and above can easily manifest money and feel comfortable around money.

Ask the question:

Angels, how can I make money stretch?

See it in your mind, physically stretching. Express delight when you buy something because you had the money for it. Also, pause before buying things; check in to see if you really want or need this. Ask the body. Tune in to the energy of the item and see how it connects to you. If you feel fearful or guilty when you buy it, it's best to wait or leave it. When you buy things in a high vibration, money works better for you.

For essential items and bills, be grateful for your ability to pay, and be very thankful for what it is you are paying for, instead of being resentful about the bill. Also, if you feel you don't have enough, be open to new options in paying for things. Is there help that you hadn't thought of? The mind contracts when it is fearful about money and "can't see the wood for the trees." Have fun making money stretch. Enjoy in childlike wonder how you can provide for yourself (and others, if applicable).

I have an abundance visualization on YouTube, in an interview with tapping guru Brad Yates in his *Get Ready* series, which goes through the 12 fifth-dimensional chakras and how they relate to abundance. Find it at **https://angeleft.com/resources**.

Make Money Your Friend

Reflect for a moment on your relationship with money. How do you feel about it? If you feel good, that is wonderful. If you don't, think for a moment about how life might be if this relationship was a good one.

*Angels, how might it be if I had a great relationship
with money?*

You feel excited about money, which is very different to being
obsessed with it. You know money is always there for you: when
you want or need something, you call money, and it comes.
Money helps you out. You place notes into your purse or wallet
with love, and when you handle money you feel calm and grateful.
You understand the exchange it represents, and it feels good.

5

Vibrant Physical Health and Food

Angels, how can I improve my physical health?

First, look at what you put into your body. On Earth, there is an opportunity to put so much light into your body through what you eat and ingest.

With the right fuel, your body has the potential to heal. See a multi-stranded approach. Health and healing on many levels. Is there something in your emotional life that your body is telling you to address? Or in the home?

The mind and body cannot be separated as some may think. The inner world and the outer world neither. As within, so without. As above, so below. See yourself as the whole-istic being that you are. Your physical body and all its many parts as a system. Your chakras, your energy meridians, your auric field and its layers. If you were to look down from above, taking a bird's-eye view of you in your life right now, how would things look? You will see more than just the parts you have previously focused on.

The Body Is Always Telling Us

Your body is a compass. It will show you which way to go. Which foods to eat. Who and what to trust. It knows yes and no if we only stop and ask it. This is also known as our intuition or gut feeling. Though I don't think for a minute it's just related to the gut. It's the whole. All of your body tells you because one part is not separated from the next.

Quite often, the symptoms or illness we experience have a message for us. For example, suffering from a chest infection can relate to grief or feeling heavy of heart since the heart is in the chest. If you are suffering from an ailment, see if you can decipher any messages the body is trying to communicate to you.

Healing the Body with Archangel Raphael

Archangel Raphael is known as the healing angel and works on an emerald-green ray. He encourages us to listen to the message the body is sending us so that we learn the lesson and don't need to keep repeating it all over again.

Take some deep, comfortable breaths. Invite Raphael's emerald healing light into every cell of the body, send it out ahead of you to guide you in your day, and ask it to infuse your food.

I have healed things in myself in the most amazing ways, simply by asking Archangel Raphael to heal me now and imagining the emerald healing light going to that part of the body.

Archangel Raphael, how can I help myself to eat light and healthy foods today?

Visualize yourself eating those healthy foods and feeling the high vibration this offers your body. You are in alignment with what you put into your body. If you prepare food today, place your loving hands on this food and put your loving energy into it. Ask the angels to bless your food and your water. A lack of presence is what has held you back in the past when you have not chosen healthy foods. Awareness will bring you back to your greatest choices. Make those foods available by buying them and having them at home, and with you when you travel and work away from home. Energize your food-making and eating space. Clean and uplift the energy of the space where you prepare food. Clean the fridge and clean out the food cupboards and the place you store eating utensils, bowls, and plates. Bless this space. Bring in a crystal and candles, and make eating sacred. Take your time. Really enjoy your food when you are hungry. Stop when you are full. Put less on your plate.

What we eat and ingest has a huge bearing on our energy fields and the life we live. If you need to take medication, hold it in your hands before you take it. Ask the angels to clear it of all lower energies and bless it with light before you put it into your body.

When I read Allen Carr's *Easy Way to Quit Emotional Eating* it made me realize how people are brainwashed to eat junk food. When you walk into any supermarket, within seconds you're presented with colourfully packaged junk and "great bargains." Yes, there's the fruit and veg aisle too, and there are healthy options, but they aren't as loud and shiny as the junk food.

Advertisements tell us that happiness can be found in eating chocolate, crisps, pizzas, fast food, and so on. Many of us associate junk food with parties and having a good time. And yet where is the truth in it, that this food makes us happier? Most of us feel worse after eating it. It puts pressure on the body, like an inner clutter. When we prepare a lovely, healthy snack or meal with our own hands, whether simple or complex, we get much more from it.

Angels, how can I rest and relax in the evenings without eating extra food?

Feel the joy in your body. Turn towards gratitude. Gratitude for
your body, for the day you've had, for the space now to relax.
Enjoy golden light flowing into the body and working its way
around every part of you. You are complete. Know that you need
to add nothing more unless it is water for hydration. You may
enjoy, for example, massaging your feet with beautiful oils. Bring
love into your body. Say, "I love you," when you look in the
mirror. Move away from any habits of criticism or conditional
love, such as, "I will love you when . . ." Rebel against the third-
dimensional paradox of being harsh on one's own appearance
and feeling unaccepted. These are mere excuses not to be
in your bliss.

EFT and Tapping for Healthy Eating

Some years ago, I created a tapping programme called Love Yourself Slim with EFT that has a wide range of audio recordings of example tapping rounds, aimed at those who struggle with overeating. This affects so many people and I believe that, when we learn to understand the problem and clear the energy, we can change the behaviour and heal our eating.

Laura, a mother of two working from home, would eat healthy food throughout the day and then in the evening begin to excessively overeat. She noticed a sudden insatiable hunger that didn't make any sense. Through tapping, she received the insight that she was overeating in the evenings to anchor herself and slow down. By day, she was rushing around, getting things done while her daughters were at school. She hadn't quite learned how to finish the working day, and so in the evening used overeating as a way to make herself "heavy" enough to slow down. The food made her tired and feel forced to sit down and stop "doing."

With this knowledge and the clearing she received from the tapping, Laura felt quite differently about food in the evenings. She no longer wished to overeat, and, if a craving suddenly spontaneously reoccurred, she used tapping to get through it. She quickly felt lighter in her body and in her being. She used the affirmation: I am anchored and grounded.

Law of Attraction

In *The Power*, Rhonda Byrne tells us that when we focus on a weight problem, over and over, we keep attracting this to us. If we can change our minds and focus on having a slim, healthy body, this can really help us to create it. She says that *envying* someone with a slim, healthy body is also telling the law of attraction that we don't want it. Instead, she says, feel joy when you see someone with this great body. The universe is showing you this because you can have it too.

You Are Beautiful

If you find yourself constantly condemning yourself for being over-weight, being undisciplined, and being addicted to junk food, you will have developed self-destructive ways that go against you naturally reaching for healthy habits. So come back to self-love first and foremost. You cannot hate yourself into healthy habits. Any punishing attempts are totally unsustainable, rather like an elastic band being stretched more and more. Eventually, it will either ping back or snap.

Practise focusing on your magnificence. If you feel you are too thin or too fat or parts of your body don't match up with what we've been shown is beautiful, know that you have a certain unique radiance that shines out of you when you smile. When you laugh. When you open your heart and love something or someone. When you intend goodness for another.

When you enter a room or a building say to yourself, *How can I shine my light here?* This is beautiful, and others will see it. Do you know someone who doesn't look aesthetically beautiful in a typical way but whose light shines so brightly they are unmistakably gorgeous? These people are showing humankind something important.

Home-Grown Food

After hurting my knee in 2021 and being unable to walk, I asked my angels, *What do I need to do to heal myself?* They said diet, as well as other things. They said that the vibration of home-grown vegetables is very high and fills the body with light. Not all of us are able to grow our own, but even if you live in a small apartment it may be possible to grow lettuce on your windowsill, for example. Alternatively, buying locally grown and organic food helps too. This is not only because of the better quality but also because the vibration of food that's been sprayed with pesticides is lower. Things that have hurt Mother Earth are lower-frequency.

If you experience financial obstacles in buying organic, healthy food, ask, *Angels, how can I include more high-frequency foods in my diet?* And then be open to what comes. Also, bless your food before you eat it. This needn't take more than a few seconds. For those of you who have trained in Reiki it is like "reiki-ing" the food or drink before you eat it; but spend as little or as much time as you like, since it's the intention that matters. You can even say when you drink anything, *Water dragons, please raise the frequency of this drink.* The effects are most noticeable. I have even experienced the taste of not very nice-tasting tap water improving.

Angel Intervention—from Despair to Healing

One day when I was still healing, I asked the angels, "Please help me. I need something now to help with my knee." I was feeling desperate; I had tried so many things but was only making very slow progress and feeling vulnerable and disabled.

That morning two things happened. I went to the supermarket and a loaf of spelt bread jumped off the shelf to my feet. I simply picked it up and put it back. I had already chosen some wheat bread and was going to stubbornly hang on to it, although I noted that this was odd and could have been a sign. Next, a man knocked at my door and told me he learned how to heal himself when he developed a chronic back issue. He spoke about wheat and the inflammation that eating wheat causes around the joints and how eating spelt instead can help. Especially if you've baked it yourself, since some of the spelt bread in the shops has wheat in it. As he spoke, rainbows began appearing behind him one after the other, and he went on to help me heal my knee.

Archangel and Dragon Visualization
Healing Your Relationship with Food and Body

1. See yourself walking into a cave edged with beautiful ferns. Little drops of water are like purifying crystal blessings. At the mouth of the cave, there are iron pyrite crystals shimmering gold all around the edges. Pause here and allow yourself to be cleansed and grounded by these beautiful gold crystals.

2. A crystal yellow dragon appears at your side, and you make a connection with her. She breathes light onto your crown chakra, helping to raise your thoughts about food and body.

3. The crystal yellow dragon tells you to climb up on her back and so you do. You feel safe and can feel light coming from her that's very soothing. You hold on and she flies into the cave, which opens out and becomes larger inside. You see many crystals of every colour.

4. Your dragon gently lands in the centre of a great dome. There are many candles, and the light is bright and magical. You see sparkles as you step onto the mossy ground.

5. Archangel Jophiel is approaching you. The mighty archangel stands before you and you feel their amazing energy flowing over you. Archangel Jophiel will, with your permission, help you to reprogramme your thoughts around food and diet to ones that will support your healthy life. You are now open to any extra help and assistance that you may require. This may come in the form of a person you meet, a conversation you overhear, a book, a course, an article, or just divine guidance being dropped into your mind.

6. Spend some time here as Archangel Jophiel works on your crown chakra.

7. Archangel Raphael comes forward now and is helping to release any old unhelpful images you have been envisioning in your third eye about yourself and food. See these being found and released into the light.

8. Archangel Raphael invites you to create a very powerful picture in your mind of you living your blissful life and eating healthy foods. You have plenty of space in your third eye now to create lots of positive images. See yourself in many different situations, enjoying foods that are healthy, or even saying no to unhealthy food that is offered, and feeling really good about your choice. Saying to yourself, Thank goodness I don't have to eat that any more. My body feels wonderful now.

9. Imagine a short clip of you in this life, like you are watching yourself on a movie screen. See yourself as joyous and happy, feeling great in your body and enjoying very beautiful high-vibrational foods.

10. Sparkling green dragons are surrounding you, and they whisper helpful information to you about what foods your body particularly loves. Which are those foods? They tell you when you include these in your diet you have more energy and feel fantastic. They are blessing your food for you from here onward. Remember to thank them.

11. When you are finished, thank the archangels and the dragons and travel with your crystal yellow dragon back to where you started.

12. Come fully back into your body. Place your hands on your heart centre. Feel the warmth flowing from your hands into your heart. Now place your hands anywhere else on the body that they are drawn to and send this area love. Thank your body for the amazing work it does for you every second of every day.

Let that gratitude for your body become a sacred habit that you return to over and over. A body that is frequently criticized is tense and retains more fluid. When you love your body and are grateful for it, your body relaxes more and it's easier to work in harmony with it.

Foods That Look Like Body Parts?

One time I had a chesty cough and was really sick with it. A friend who is very psychic told me she had received a message from the angels for me to eat broccoli. I remembered that broccoli is good for the lungs, and I got some and prepared a lovely stir-fry with it. I told her this, and she hadn't realized, she was just given the message to pass on.

Quite often, food that heals a certain part of the body looks a bit like that part. The little branches of broccoli look a bit like the bronchioles in the lungs, for example. Walnuts are good for the brain. Tomato is said to be good for heart health as tomatoes have four chambers just like the heart. Avocado is shaped like the uterus and is known for supporting good uterine health. Celery is good for the bones. And so on.

Your Nourishing Foods

Make a list of foods that you already know are really nourishing for you. Ask the angels, are there any more?

6

Perfect Job

Angels, how do I manifest my perfect job?

See yourself doing it and loving it. Imagine it with all your heart. In our perfect job, we don't feel like we're working because we love it so much. It feels like "I was born to do this." My wish is for every person to do that which lights them up and brings joy. I didn't always work in my dream job, although I'm hugely grateful for every job I've had, since I've learned so much through all of them.

If you're not sure what your ideal job is, ask: *Angels, what is a great job for me?*

Mind Map

Do you want to work from home, by yourself or among others, in an office, or outside in nature? What are the hobbies that you enjoy? What makes you feel switched on in life? What gives you a buzz or a jolt of happiness in your soul?

Get a piece of paper or turn to a page of your journal and write in the centre in a bubble "jobs I could love." Now make a mind map by jotting down ideas that flow into your mind. Don't think too hard. Ask the angels to send ideas through you. Loosen your hand as you write so words can flow easily.

Be an Open Channel

Now you've got your mind map you should have a bit more clarity. But whether you do or you don't, if you've asked the question, trust that the answer is on its way. Be aware of thoughts that drop into your mind.

Notice what you enjoy doing. Be playful and get excited, knowing that your perfect dream job is out there and each time you have a joyful thought about it you are bringing it closer.

Don't be afraid to reach out to experts if appropriate. There are psychometric tests for career suitability that some careers counsellors can work on with you. Or there are various career quizzes you can complete online yourself that can offer clarity or ideas. You could ask:

Angels, how can I leave my old job and transition perfectly to a job I love?

I would never advise someone to leap into the unknown, leaving a financially secure job. Instead, knowing that things have the potential to move in ways you have never imagined, take the steps necessary to manifest your dream job and stay open. When you are in a regular dialogue with the angels, you find yourself on a golden path where doors keep opening. Watch your thoughts and language.

Stay Awake and Be Curious

Everyone's situation is unique, but, if you keep asking and stay alert and curious to possibility, you can expect the answer to drop into your life. It is a third-dimensional thought that we can't possibly leave a job that we're unhappy in because we'll not receive enough from the universe in any other way. And yet that thought can be pushed onto us by those around us, or by ourselves.

How about changing the narrative for yourself by using an affirmation? Combining tapping with affirmations can be incredibly powerful. Two powerful affirmations are:

- I am so grateful to be in my perfect job.

- I love that I wake each morning with joy and excitement.

Create the Feeling

Imagine you're working in your perfect job. Don't worry if you're still not clear about what or where it is. Instead, create the feeling. What does it feel like to do the work of your dreams? Your heart should be overflowing with joy. It doesn't feel like work at all because you love doing it and would do this for free. And yet now you have plenty of money and are in prosperity consciousness.

Avoid affirmations that say my perfect new job is coming to me—instead talk about it like it's happening *now*. Saying things that pop into your mind about your fabulous new job is a powerful way to anchor this feeling and vibrational match to what you're seeking.

The Angels Know What's for You and What's Not

Some years ago, I went for a job within the organization I worked in at the time. I felt quite sure I would love the position. Just one colleague and I went for the job, and I had no problem visualizing that I had got this post. I thanked my angels for the job, and when the interview happened I thought it went well. Driving to town, I even saw an angel-shaped cloud in the sky, and I thought, "This is more confirmation that I have got the job."

I didn't end up getting it. Even though my colleague was a suitable choice, I was surprised and couldn't understand it. I had visualized getting it so clearly in my mind! Yet later, the colleague told me the job was terrible, and he was having trouble getting out of it. Things weren't as they seemed.

This demonstrates well how the angels can see things that we can't. They know what's for our highest good. If I had got the job I would have learned that lesson also—that sometimes what we're chasing isn't for us. Not long afterwards, I was promoted to a much more suitable role and was hugely grateful.

Love Yourself Into the New

You can't resent yourself out of a job, home, area, or anything else. You need to raise your vibration so high that you are no longer a match for the place you are at and will simply be propelled out of it and on to somewhere that you fit.

Try asking:

Angels, how do I improve things at my current job?

If you work in a place that you want to stay in but that has problems, there is a lot you can do to help. Years ago, working as a nurse, I knew that this wasn't my dream job and I'd rather help people in other ways, but I still enjoyed it and had no intention of leaving at that time. I used to spend my long walk down the corridor asking the angels to bring light into my aura. I could see colours begin to swirl and build in my auric field, sometimes patterns and symbols too. I trusted that this was perfect for my day, and later in the day I would understand why those colours, shapes, patterns, and symbols were there. Certain situations would arise at work and I would understand why those things were relevant. The angels use many different ways to show us things and help us.

Open the Door—Whatever You Think, You Are Right

Things can start to improve in miraculous ways when you bring the angelic realms into your job by asking them for assistance. Have fun and be creative. If you are open to miracles and wonderful things happening, you have opened a door to let them in. If, however, you have decided what can and can't happen, what's possible and impossible, you are right. In other words, that is what you will create.

Archangel Michael's Deep Blue Dragons

Archangel Michaels's deep blue dragons are powerful helpers. Ask them to fly down under the building of your workplace, or if there isn't a physical base ask them to fly into the computers and the energy of the organization. They are fiercely protective and can break up the densest of energies. See them lighting and clearing the way ahead of you and around you. Ask one to stay at your side, or a number of them to stay around you. They will be there for you.

Unicorns in the Workplace

Ask the unicorns to touch every person in your workplace today. See them in your mind's eye spreading light around the building, office, or through the internet. By regularly visualizing the angelic realms supporting you, you will notice a change in energy. Sometimes it is this very change that makes it possible for you to see your next step.

7

Delightful Home

Angels, how do I manifest my dream home?
Be clear about your dream home. Feel what it is like to live there.
Now love yourself into it.

What is your dream home? Are you already living where you want to live but just want it to be tidier, and decorated better, or do you want to move? Are you living in a place that is far from your dream home? Go to the vibrational scale on page 21 and measure how your home feels now on the scale.

We are often fed the idea that a dream home must be enormous and cost a lot of money, while in reality it's a home that you feel at home in. A home that you love waking up in, going to bed in, dining in, and doing whatever else you love to do in it. Does your home have a garden? What is the light like inside your home? What are the views like? Who are your neighbours, if you have any? What's in the vicinity? You could ask:

Archangel Raphael, what is my dream home like?

> ### Connecting with Your Dream Home
>
> Close your eyes and imagine walking around your dream home, from room to room. Your angels are with you, lighting up each room as you go.
>
> Look out of the windows and notice what you see. Again, this may be the home you are already in but looking and feeling just how you want it to be.

The Chakras and Decluttering

Typically, in the chakra system clutter is associated with the base chakra, but it can also engage others, such as holding grief in the heart chakra; you may hold on to something because the thought of getting rid of it gives you a pain in your heart. For this reason, notice your bodily sensations when you are going through your things. Whereabouts in the body can you feel that heavy energy or ache, for example? Often, it's connected to the chakra closest to this area. A headache might be related to the crown chakra and your thoughts, or what you are visualizing in your third eye. Lower-abdomen heaviness could relate to the sacral chakra. Below the heart, the solar plexus chakra tells us when we are feeling fear or anxiety or disempowerment, for example. The throat is for expression and blocked or thwarted creativity, such as finding an unfinished manuscript and wondering what to do with it, or old business cards that sat in a drawer.

Jane's Story of the Energy of Stuff

Over the years Jane struggled with clutter. Having too many things and lacking a good system for organizing them. Difficulty moving things on that could do with a clear-out. Her dream home was the one she was living in, only tidy and free of clutter. Both she and her partner tended to hoard things. "I find it difficult even to throw away an envelope," she told me. This issue kept coming back to her for years until she really put the energy in to change it. We did some Angel EFT on having a tidy home and many other issues came up as we did so. It was as though each area of clutter had its own emotional story in her life. As we went around each one and cleared the issue, she was able to go home and begin clearing that area. Angel EFT involves tapping on energy meridian endpoints while engaging the angelic realms for extra support.

Jane also listened to my dragon workshop *"Make Your Home a Portal of Light,"* and from this she learned where the chakras of her home were. She took time to connect with them all daily for 21 days, and after three months there was a huge difference in her home. I met her some months later and she was beaming. "My house is like a completely different world," she told me. Jane explained how not only had she changed her habits and was able to easily keep the house tidy, let things go and not hoard clutter, but that it had a knock-on effect on her partner. She was resistant at first but then, liking the tidiness, sought her own help with hoarding. "And now the house is clear, bright, and beautiful," she told me. "A real portal of light—and my dream home."

Decluttering—One Thing at a Time

If you have been dealing with a clutter issue, try starting with one small area at a time. To help me break through procrastination, I like to set a timer for 25 minutes (inspired by the Pomodoro Technique, as described on page 213). For just 25 minutes, start to clear an area of your home. Perhaps it's a table or drawer, or a pile of clothes. See what you can get done before the time runs out. Wondering where to begin? Try asking: *Archangel Gabriel, where is best for me to start?*

Do the same again tomorrow. Each day, do 25 minutes. Or more, or less, according to what you can afford to put in. Setting the timer gets me out of my head and into my body. I can get on and move easier when there's nothing to do apart from get on with the focused task at hand. See page 184 for more on decluttering.

Upgrading the Home You Are In

If it's the case that you like your current home, but it needs repairs or upgrades, you can work on cultivating this energetically as well. Try your best to love your home just as it is, while also seeing its beauty unfolding, like a flower. If you look around your home with eyes of disdain, it won't flourish and grow easily. Just like a child who's not doing well in school, approval and kindness is what helps.

Think of your home as a living thing. Because in a way, it is. Your home is energy, and it is very connected to you and your energy. If you love it and are grateful for your home, it's easier to work with it in making improvements.

Manifesting the Money

If whatever you need to do to your home, or moving to a new one, requires money, work on your prosperity consciousness. How prosperous do you feel on the scale right now? If you're at 10, you won't be worried at all about how you can afford to make those changes. If you are at 0, you are as far away from that feeling as possible—in fact, it feels impossible. Go back to Chapter 4: (page 49) if you need to.

To manifest money for a particular project, focus on already having the money. Tune in to your delight at having enough. Feel relieved and joyful at being able to make those changes. If you feel doubtful or conflicted, you need to bring your prosperity consciousness up on the scale. In the higher numbers, we are open to the money coming from anywhere, we are open to miracles, and we know that there's more than this too. If we need money for something else afterwards, that can be manifested also. This is different to someone who is irresponsible with money and spends it unwisely, which is a denial behaviour coming from the fearful lower end of the scale.

On the higher end of the scale, you are responsible, and you also attract miracles.

Dream Home Angel Visualization

1. Feel your guardian angel approaching you. Notice how they connect with you. Do they surround you, or touch your shoulder blades with great hands of light? Or do you just notice the feeling of love they bring?

2. Your guardian angel is guiding you through the dimensions. You land in front of your dream home and your guardian angel is giving you the key. You open the door. Step inside and notice how it smells. The beautiful sparkling energy. Greet the home, say hello. Many angels are inside and are coming to greet you too, as well as the angel of this home.

3. Feel the way it welcomes you. The joy you experience as you walk from room to room. Touch the surfaces and the furniture. See yourself using each room as you would like to. Take a seat in one of the rooms. This room is filling up with light and many angels are coming to your side. They love to see that you are here in your dream home.

Love the Home You Are in to Move to a Better One

If you want to move out of the home you are in into a better one, you must love the one you're in in order to move. You simply can't hate or begrudge your way out of your current home into a better one. It doesn't work that way. Use powerful targeted questions to the angels to help raise your frequency so high that you are no longer a good fit for the current home. This will help you to manifest yourself into a better one that correlates with your higher energy.

Gold, Silver, and Violet Flame Dragons to Purify Your Home

You can ask the gold, silver, and violet flame dragons to purify your home, whether it's in the one you are in now or the one you hope or plan to move to. It helps to clear the energies and make the very best of them.

Visualization with the Gold, Silver, and Violet Flame Dragons

1. Invoke the gold, silver, and violet flame dragons. Feel them surrounding you now.

2. Ask them to fill your home with your light.

3. See them flying around it and under its foundations. They easily and powerfully clear the energy of the place.

4. See them going into each room and using their gold, silver, and violet fire to clear away any lower-frequency energies.

5. Allow your breathing to relax as you notice the change in the atmosphere of your home. It feels more peaceful, and clearer.

6. See the dragons moving around you. Helping you in each room that you use. Clearing objects, devices, and other people in the home. Clearing thoughts.

7. See everything and everyone feeling better and brighter.

8. Now ask the dragons to purify your energy fields and expand your aura brightly and vastly. You are a good influence on your home. You bring your light into each room and everywhere you go.

9. Does your home have a message for you? What does it say? Make a note of it so you can work with this. Thank the dragons.

10. Bring your awareness back to the physical location where you started.

8

Creative Bliss

Angels, how can I enjoy my creativity fully in my life?

What are you permitting for yourself right now? What do you want to allow, and enjoy in your life? If you were living your best life, how would creativity look? Tune in, to know where in your body your creativity is. Sometimes we feel it in our hands, in our core, in our heart, or elsewhere. Does it feel stuck or free-flowing? What does it want to say to you?

It took me from childhood to being over 40 to finish my first novel. I started many of them over the years, and rarely reached the halfway mark of a first draft. Something would block me. Fear. Doubt. A book in progress felt safer than a book that was finished. If it's in progress you don't have to stand by it as such, since it's unfinished and can get better. A part of you knows that this potentially wonderful book is inside of you, but how to excavate it? This experience applies to all manner of creative projects.

I believe that everyone is creative, but not everyone thinks so. Not everyone resonates with the word, and yet our creativity is the magic in our hands, the things we make, fix, and express. I have met many people who got the message that creative pursuits are frivolous, self-indulgent, or foolish. In my work, I have met many people who have come into balance by allowing their creativity to blossom. Even if you don't see yourself working in your favourite creative field, giving some time to it for leisure, for fun, or as a side project can improve your life on so many levels.

The Sacral Chakra and Creativity

When our creativity is stuck or buried inside of us it can manifest as a blockage in the sacral chakra, which is also where our sexual energy is housed. It is no surprise that our creative force then is like life force. When it is stunted, we don't feel truly alive. There are so many ways you can enjoy using your creativity.

Being Creative

Write down the ways you love to be creative. Then stretch a little further. Think of more things.

Here are just a few examples:

Gardening, cooking, projects, home decor, candle making, building a shed/den/treehouse, flower arranging, sewing or making clothes or any items by hand, music, making a stone wall, photography, acting; singing, dancing, rearranging, painting stones, pottery . . .

Allow your creativity to flow and feel joy in your life. As a writer, I am happy when I am writing every day. I would feel some trepidation if I was asked to draw or paint something, and yet I keep an open mind. I have attended art classes and ended up loving it, even though it doesn't feel as comfortable and fluid to me as writing. I am open to new ways of being creative.

Archangel Gabriel, how can I help to release my creative self today and be in flow?

Dear One, did you think you were just this body? You are an entire universe, you cannot imagine how vast. You are connected to an infinite creative flow that you can channel any time you open up to it. Listen to the murmurs of your soul. What excites you and makes you feel alive? Connect and be open.

Opportunities to create don't only come when you are in your field of creating, they come at all times throughout the day. Creative thought can come in many ways. Even asking questions such as these is a form of your creativity manifesting. Invent games to access your highest flow. Be in tune with it. This is the Source energy flowing through you. Your *I Am* presence, and not something frivolous. Look all around you and see how many colours you can see. Notice how the light plays, what energies you feel, what magic you can tap into.

Self-Doubt and Creativity

Angels, how can I overcome my inner critic,
so I am free to . . . (name creative pursuit)?

Play, play, and play some more. The inner critic as you call it
comes from an external place—a memory from younger years.
And from the ego; your hurt shadow side. It has no power over
you. Come back to your curiosity. Stay open. Just as when
someone gives you bad advice you have the choice to let it go,
likewise you can do so with this critical voice.

You were made to do these things; your soul vibrates at a very high frequency when you allow yourself to play. Give yourself permission to make mistakes and not worry about doing things to a high standard, which is the fuel for your inner critic. It is not important to get things perfectly right. In fact, to get good, we often need to make mistakes. The shame and fear you experience when feeling stuck or unable to create is the untruth that you can learn to tune out. Create to reach the higher notes and to improve. Think of your favourite artist and what you might say to them if they told you they were too full of self-doubt to create those things that you love so much.

Cathal often dreamed of writing short stories, but when he sat down to have a go he was plagued by memories of being at school and a teacher's red pen all over his English work. He couldn't get those disparaging remarks out of his mind whenever he tried to write. The boy beside him always got top marks and yet no matter how hard he tried he barely passed, always getting low marks and plenty of critical feedback.

Together, we looked at how to move past this so Cathal would be able to write with ease and joy. We called upon Archangel Gabriel to guide him. He received the instruction loud and clear: forgive and move on. He thought of the teacher, a much older man now, and felt compassion for him. He understood that by holding on to resentment, he was tethered to the past and the teacher. This was halting his progress.

To change the negative narrative in his mind, Cathal also began to use the phrase, "I am a good enough writer." Saying to himself "I am a brilliant writer" wasn't a good choice as it put him under pressure. As a good enough writer, he could write without worry or self-criticism and enjoy himself. A month later he emailed me to say he had sent off a short story to five places. Not minding too much about winning or getting published, Cathal was just delighted to have finished a story and was already working on two more.

Many creatives have stories of being held back or put down in the past. Someone in authority or who was important to them said something hurtful or discouraging about their art and they shrank in and closed down. Julia Cameron in her famous *Artist's Way* programme talks about this and forgiving where possible so you can fully move on. If this resonates for you, try asking Ascended Master Quan Yin:

Dear Quan Yin, how may I be more forgiving now of this past pain so that I feel free to create?

Visualization with the Fire Dragons
Changing an Old Story (Limiting Belief)

1. Ground yourself by sending down energy roots that flow through your legs and feet, through the floor, and into the earth below. Send them deep down into Mother Earth.

2. Send light from your heart up to Source and feel Source responding by pouring an abundance of golden rainbow light over you. This light flows down generously through your stellar gateway chakra, the soul star, the causal, the crown, the third eye, the throat, the heart, the solar plexus, the navel, the sacral, the base, and the earth star chakra beneath your feet. Feel your energy levels rising.

3. Invoke a fire dragon. See them blazing before you, shimmering with their powerful etheric fire. The dragon is a loving being come to help you with this task of rewriting an old story you feel has inhibited your creativity.

4. Tell them about the old story—an unpleasant memory or limiting belief formed in your past that stops you from expressing your creativity. The dragon listens with their big, loving, fiery heart open wide.

5. See the story floating before you, detaching itself and becoming a thought form hovering in front of you. Notice its shape and colour.

6. With your permission, the fire dragon breathes its powerful fire of transmutation to dissolve the story now. Take some deep breaths as they do this. The energy and effects of the story are being blazed up into the light.

7. The dragon asks you to tell the new story now. So you are free to create a new story for that past aspect of you. Perhaps if it was unkind words, an advocate steps in and revokes the comment or speaks to the person involved, making them see and change their comments. Or maybe the younger version of you can respond with the strength needed and doesn't take what was said or done to heart. Or a host of angels surround this earlier version of you, removing all the pain of what was said or done and all its effects. Take some time for this.

8. The fire dragon breathes a much gentler form of fire now that has a beautiful colour, energizing the new story. They encourage you to take this story and place it in your heart, and from there it radiates around all of your energy bodies and chakras as you fully accept it.

9. Feel into your new, free, creative self.

10. Thank the fire dragon and come back into your body fully, remembering your grounding. Stretch and drink some water.

11. Ask yourself, what would I like to create today? Have fun doing something creative.

A Life That Shimmers

Angels, how can I live the life of my dreams?

Pause to reflect on all the dreams that have already come true
in your life. See them glowing and expanding. See them grow
brighter until they stretch and touch those other dreams you still
have. See yourself bathed in light, bursting with joy. Return to
this image so that it is imprinted in your consciousness.

What answer did you receive? Make notes. What is the life of your
dreams? Take out a piece of paper and brainstorm that life. Be curious
and playful and write down whatever comes into your head.

- What themes come up the most?
- What did you learn from doing that?

You may find that there are many headings. I also like the wheel of life for
this exercise (see Chapter 3, page 40, and **https://angeleft.com/resources**
for download). Write a heading for each slice that relates specifically to
the life of your dreams. Here are some ideas for the headings you might
choose; or you might be inspired by them but pick your own.

- Love Relationship
- Money & Prosperity
- My Amazing Job
- Spiritual Life
- Fun & Adventure
- Happy Body and Exercise

- Creative Fun

- Helping Mother Earth

- Awesome Friends

- Chill Time—Connect with Self

- Connecting with/diving into Nature

- Delicious Food

Is it similar or different to the one you made in Chapter 3, if you made one? You can make your wheel much more focused. For example, if you wanted to devote an entire wheel to a project that is very important to you, you can do that. Or your romantic relationship. What are the finer aspects of these?

Then in your wheel, you can make ten levels to grade each segment. So, 0 out of 10 would be like 0 on the vibrational scale—each number corresponds. Where are you on the vibrational scale with each segment? And what matters the most? This tells you what to focus on today. For example, if one segment is coming out at a 4 and another is a 6 but that segment is much more important, start with that. You can come back to the other one later.

Archangel Metatron's Cube

Archangel Metatron is overseeing the ascension process on Earth and the universe and his energy is golden-orange, but you may perceive it as any colour, depending on how this mighty archangel chooses to connect with you.

Metatron works with sacred geometry and his cube (see overleaf) is very powerful. I like to have it in my office space, on the wall, or in other places where I can see it and connect with it. Sometimes I place it under physical things in my home, asking that his beautiful energy touches whatever it is.

Just by looking at the Metatron Cube, you are connecting with the vibration of Metatron. This vibration encapsulates very powerful sacred codes that you can receive and activate within your life and energy fields.

Ask for Metatron to bless your wheel of life (or brainstorm list) and raise its frequency. Print the cube and stick it to the back of your wheel to help bring Metatron's energy in and purify any areas that have felt stagnant or that need a boost.

On the next page I am offering a prayer to Archangel Metatron; you can use this or create your own prayer.

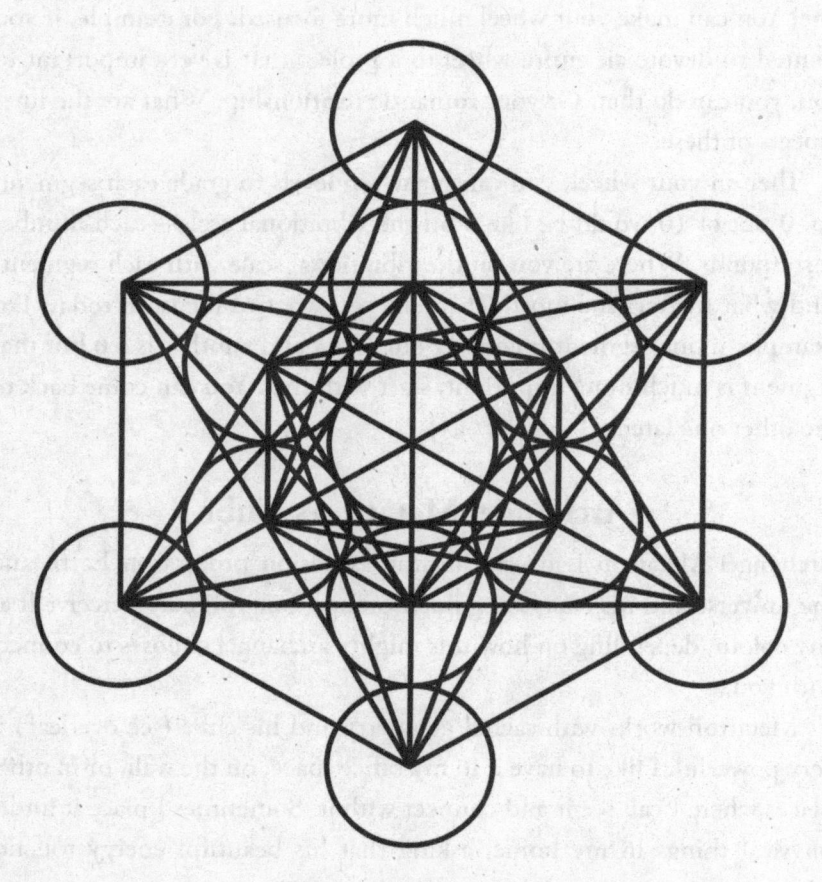

Fig.3: Metatron's Cube

> *Dear Archangel Metatron,*
> *Help me to live the life of my dreams. The life I came here for. Let me fully realize my potential and spread my wings now. I am a light bearer and came to help others to expand too. Fill me up with light so that I can really shine now.*
>
> *Help me to step into my power. My success inspires others and helps others. Guide me on my next steps and help me to feel the joy in this. I open myself up to your light.*
> *Amen. So It Is.*

Feel Archangel Metatron placing his cloak of light around you. Take some deep breaths as you connect with its energy. Your whole aura is shimmering brightly, and you can be seen by angels and masters everywhere. Smile and acknowledge them.

Telling New Stories About Your Life

What stories are you telling yourself and others about your life now? Start to pay attention. If you aren't telling of your amazing life but of how unhappy or dissatisfied you are, then you are not attracting this wonderful life you say you'd like. If your life seems full of problems, it can be a challenge, but do your best to speak mostly about what's going well or what you're grateful for and excited about.

Other people are our greatest teachers in staying on track with this. If those around you speak negatively, you need to work twice as hard to stay positive and not get pulled into negative talk. Remember though that it works both ways. Your speaking more positively will also help to inspire others to do the same. And if you ignite the inspiration in just one person to be more positive and thus attract good things, this also comes back to you in many ways. You receive what you give out, so delight in helping others to be more positive and raise their vibration also.

Positive Outlook vs. Toxic Positivity

Toxic positivity is where a person refuses to acknowledge another's (or their own) suffering or a difficult situation because they are insisting on "being positive." You will notice the difference between this and having a positive outlook. Toxic positivity—the clue is in the name—feels toxic. It can be passive-aggressive, disempowering, and a way to stop people from expressing their truth.

The difference is that a genuine bright disposition is empathic and kind in nature and you can listen to others with an open heart. It's okay to say you are struggling and ask for help, and likewise to listen with compassion if someone else needs to express their pain. The lesson is to keep reaching for the higher thought and asking questions, so . . . "what can I do to help myself with this? What's the best course of action for me right now?"

Poor Thing

Nora had a friend who was always in the victim role. She complained all the time, and, to Nora, perhaps rightly so. Her life seemed very hard. She was older than Nora, didn't get along with her partner, and had many aches and pains. "You poor thing," Nora would say to her, but it didn't feel like a helpful thing to say. Nora came away feeling drained. She was fond of her friend, so she didn't want to end the friendship, but she wondered if she could respond differently.

We looked at alternative ways in which to respond. Nora came up with the thought, after addressing the question to Archangel Michael, to ask her friend more questions. She stopped feeling sorry for her all the time and found a way to compassionately put the onus back on her.

"I wonder what you could do to feel better around this."
"What do you think might help the situation?"
"Is there something else you might try?"

Quite soon, her friend was complaining much less, and then she stopped. Nora no longer felt drained, and her friend even laughed and smiled more. Nora felt freer to be herself, and their exchanges were enjoyable.

Eavesdrop on Your Own Conversation

Get used to listening to yourself, as if you were eavesdropping on your own conversation. *How am I doing just now?* Ask yourself, as you hear yourself talking about your life, your family, your job, your home, your habits, your hobbies, your passions, your anything at all. Are your words supporting your happiness and success?

Write a letter to an old friend about your amazing life

1. Recall an old school friend. Maybe one you didn't spend too much time with but quite liked, so you are not too distracted by the memories. Choose someone you haven't seen in years.

2. Ask their guardian angel, in your mind, if it's okay to do this exercise with them, remotely, without them having to know. If you receive a yes, ask Archangel Michael to protect both of you and remove any cords afterwards. If you don't receive a yes, choose someone else until you find the right person, or instead you can write to an imaginary person.

3. Imagine they have written to you, out of the blue, telling you all about how they're doing. They are living the life of their dreams and feeling on top of the world, and they just thought of you and wondered how you are doing. They've asked you all about your life now.

4. Spend some time opening your heart and being happy for them.

5. Now write them a letter thanking them and tell them how delighted you are to hear they're doing so well. Now tell them about you. Tell them that you are living your dream life and are happy on every level. Tell them where you live, what you're doing, anyone you live with, your daily activities, hobbies, work if you work, and so on. Have fun with this and allow yourself some time to complete it properly.

6. Keep the letter if you like, or release it, asking the angels to help you to manifest and create those things.

7. You have the key to changing things in your life. Think of one action you can take today to help yourself to move closer to that life you described in the letter and write that down.

Create a Vision Board

Create a vision board using the letter you wrote to inspire you. A vision board can be drawing pictures or words on paper of the things you'd like to manifest or achieve in your life. Or it could be cuttings from a magazine or printings from images from the internet. Or you can make a digital one online and either print it or use it as your screensaver or wallpaper on your devices, so you see it a lot. Some people even make moving images and videos for their vision board.

Be as creative and bold as you like. I have a blog on how to make and use vision boards that you can find on my website: **https://angeleft.com/resources**

Once I made a vision board and on it I placed an image of a beautiful cave I had seen on the internet. I didn't even know what country it was in. Later, on a family holiday in Portugal, I saw a sign saying, "Boat trip to sea caves: Algar de Benagil."! There was the cave I had on my vision board. Of course, I went to visit it. It showed me just how magical vision boards are. If you make one, spend time each day looking at it and really embracing the wonderful feelings, as though those things are in place already. The more you create that feeling the more magnetic you become for them to come into being.

The Delight in Being of Service

We are happiest when we are serving. No matter what age, everyone prefers to feel that they are helping or contributing in some way. This doesn't mean we are like slaves who never relax or do anything just for ourselves. It means we seek the meaningfulness of being part of something and connected. We like to put our gifts and abilities to use. We each want to matter and make a difference.

If you unexpectedly came into a huge sum of money and were told you never need to work a day in your life ever again and could sail around the world endlessly, eating and drinking whatever you wanted and never having to worry about anything . . . would this be the life of your dreams? For some, it can sound fun, but after a time it might get repetitive and unsatisfying, because we are here to contribute something and to give our light. Lightworkers know this instinctively. They light up when they are healing and helping others. But I believe every human is naturally like this, whether they identify with being a lightworker or not.

Again and again, come back to vibration. Check your vibrational scale that you have printed out, or look back to the one in Chapter 1. The higher you are on that scale, the easier everything becomes. At 10, no matter what your circumstances, you are already living the life of your dreams as your consciousness can perceive and feel nothing less. It also makes you a magnet for great things.

PART THREE
ANGELS AND WELL-BEING

Lovely Shadow

Bringing the Shadow into the Light

An important part of our soul growth is to recognize and befriend our shadow side. I was listening to an interview with a wise healer I recently met, and she was explaining how in the spiritual community there can be this kind of bypassing of the shadow side. Fear and denial of it. This is not healthy. Rather like toxic positivity, so it is unhealthy to disallow, or try to disown, our shadow. We simply can't anyway. And anything we try to hide or deny will grow.

The shadow part of us demonstrates our more uncomfortable emotions: envy, paranoia, negativity, vengefulness, victimhood, and the like. Naturally, we don't want to grow these things, or give them too much time and attention, without coming back to what we love. I teach tapping clients to have a "rant tap" if they need to. That is, if the shadow is talking or ranting, tap and say what shadow is saying. Let shadow be as ugly and unpleasant as it likes so it can harmlessly let off steam.

Don't try telling shadow to write a gratitude list. It won't because it can't, or, if it does try, it'll feel so resentful and fake that it's unlikely to do you any good. Remember that, just as the clouds reshape and move on, as sure as the tide goes in and out, we soon feel differently. And when it's out of your system and you feel better, you can move your focus back to what you love, what you're creating, and what you're grateful for.

Shadow and Creativity

Once when I was going through a tough time and feeling down, I took my camera down to the beach. I was doing one of those black-and-white photography challenges that was going around, where you take a picture every day for a few days and then nominate someone else to partake as well. It was a nice distraction from the difficulties that were happening around me. I took a photo of the tide coming in, the rocks and the beach, and, when I converted it into mono, I loved the photo. It seemed to express the pain I was in, but in a cathartic way. I printed and framed the photo and still love it. It reminds me of overcoming challenge and the way nature beautifully reflects back to us. Sometimes you can use creativity to express your shadow safely and healthily. Be open to this.

Angels and Our Shadows

The angels don't judge us because of our shadow aspect—they get it. If you need healing or help, then seek it. We each have wounds, even those people who seem to have a perfect life, the perfect childhood, and no problems in the earthly world. That is part of the deal of the human incarnation. Don't ignore your shadow. Recognize its voice when it speaks. Give it love and reassurance. Teach it the tools it needs.

Scary Shadows

For some people, it feels as though shadow hijacks them, as they do destructive things when shadow is in the driving seat. Maybe shadow seems to propel the person into dangerous addictive behaviours, or saying or doing damaging things. In these cases, there is often more of a wound, and greater support and help is needed. Ask, "St Germain, how best can I heal myself? What do I need to overcome this?" Or, "Show me a sign of what or who can help me."

Sanat Kumara's Aqua-Blue Light

Ascended Master Sanat Kumara has gifted us his crystal ascension blue light that will hold you if you need it. If you are distressed, triggered, angry, and feeling worried about what you might do, ask:

Sanat Kumara, please come to me now.
Hold me secure and safe in your aqua-blue crystal light
for the highest good of all.
Help to still my emotions now so that I can know what
to do to help the situation.
Let me not act until I am clear.
So be it.

Feel the light surrounding and holding you. It keeps you still, rather like being in a gel or jelly. Breathe and feel the love and support. Sanat Kumara will hold you still for as long as you need, and when you are ready he releases you, but still holds you in that light, aqua colour.

Helping Shadow with Archangel Michael's Deep Blue Dragons

1. Become aware of your breath and see a thread of light running right through you from the heart of Mother Earth all the way up to Source. This light runs through you no matter what, and nothing can sever or dim it, no matter how bad you feel. See it glowing when you acknowledge it.

2. Call in Archangel Michael's Deep Blue Dragons to assist you now.

3. See them weaving a great ball of deep blue light that they hold you in as they fly all around you. They still and hover, and all at the same time they breathe deep blue fire over you that dissolves fear. Take some deep breaths and absorb this.

4. Now see them dispersing and flying off in different directions. You might ask them to fly to certain memories in your past, or fears you have, or anger, worry, or upset. See them breathing their fire over the people, situations, or events. Open yourself to relaxation as you release some of the tension these things have been causing you.

5. Acknowledge any remaining strong shadow emotions if there are any. Know that the dragons have done important work with you.

6. One of the dragons returns before you and tells you their name—they are here to help you any time you need it, no matter how strong your shadow feels; they can cope with it and aren't afraid of it.

7. Ask them if there is anything you need to know to support yourself.

8. Thank all the dragons and come back into full awareness of your own body. If you received a name for your deep blue dragon, write it down so you can remember it and call on it when you like. Ask it to help your shadow.

The Shadow Whisperer

Just like there are animal whisperers, we can learn to become shadow whisperers, for ourselves and for others. We know that when someone does something unkind they are acting from their shadow—and that some people operate from shadow more than others! But having this awareness helps us to have more compassion and to hold these situations more gracefully for the other and ourselves.

How do you like to be treated if you are in shadow? I think most of us would appreciate the patience and understanding of others, and for those nearest to us to know this isn't really who we are. We're just having a moment or a bad day or phase. So, it is helpful in the world to know this about others. Strangers included, where we've no point of reference and we've only seen them so far as "that aggressive other driver," or "the hostile person on the phone."

Sometimes our shadow gets activated by another person's shadow, as we are triggered. Know when shadow is talking to shadow, because this awareness allows you to understand better what is happening and so opens you to more choices. Think of the shadow side as a contraction, and our light self as an expansion. And that, coming back to the scale, the lower we are on the scale on page 21, the more we are operating in shadow. So it is for everybody else. Some people don't know any of the skills to help themselves that you have.

If someone is treating you badly, know that they are operating in shadow, and they are showing you something important. Perhaps it's the lesson of recognizing the shadow in others and how to respond. Perhaps it's that you need to stand your ground and be assertive. Or that you need to walk away from a situation that has been draining you. Or that you can respond calmly even if you have been in a habit of acting on "hot thoughts" or have typically had knee-jerk reactions in the past. Only you will know the lesson that is being presented, but remember to ask, "Angels, what is this person showing me just now?"

If your shadow is activated and cannot comprehend asking the angels, instead ask, "Shadow, what are you showing me right now?" Be prepared for an answer that sounds less like the angels, yet you might be pleasantly surprised. Either way, it's good to ask. Shadow likes to be heard.

The Shadow and the Inner Child

I like the metaphor that we each have an inner child who we can connect with and support. Just like the shadow, the inner child can need healing, acceptance, warmth, and understanding. I am sure they are inextricably linked. While in therapeutic circles you typically hear people speak about healing the inner child and relating it to trauma, the inner child also has the potential for great joy and childlike wonder.

I am quite aware of my inner child when I write stories and fiction. When it's going well and I am "in" the story, I can almost feel her cartwheeling around in sheer delight. Ask your inner child what they need to feel delight, if you don't know already. It might be a hobby that you love, or being out in nature, or in the sea. When we feed our inner child with joy, we are also helping the shadow.

Other People's Shadow

The shadow of other people can spark off and awaken our shadow. When someone is talking in fear, as we saw in Chapter 9 under the heading Positive Outlook vs. Toxic Positivity, it can be unhelpful to try to coax them into speaking more positively. Instead, sometimes in these cases, work on purifying your energy right then and there. Ask Archangel Metatron, *Please work through me now. Protect me with your golden cloak of light. Hold me in your cube. Let me radiate your light so others can feel it too.* Don't worry about the words, just send the intention to Archangel Metatron or an angel, archangel, or loving being you choose. Focus on being a loving presence. You don't really need to say anything at all. Let your body speak the words, *I can hear you are in pain, and I wish you kindness and love.*

One of the biggest challenges here is not to collude, agree, or encourage. It can be tricky, especially for empaths, not to do so. In the lower states, the empath can be a people-pleaser, and sell out their own beliefs to placate others. But this is just another lesson. Keep your integrity.

Imagine that you are a great master of light, listening to the pain and shadow of a precious soul who is feeling fearful. Think of how you—your higher self—would like others to respond if you are acting in shadow and speaking a low-frequency dialogue.

> *Archangel Metatron, please work through me now.*
> *Protect me with your golden cloak of light.*
> *Hold me in your sacred cube.*
> *Radiate your light through me.*
> *Amen. So It Is.*

11

Releasing the Grip of Anxiety

Anxiety is always telling us something. Where it has become habitual, we can retrain the mind in order to create new thoughts and feelings. So how might we do this? It's often unclear where anxiety comes from unless it's associated with post-traumatic stress. Perhaps it's genetic; or, rather, passed on through the ancestral lineage as an unresolved trauma. Maybe it's coming from a fear base in the collective consciousness. The possibilities are vast. Perhaps more helpfully than going on a quest to know where it originates from, we can simply learn how to respond to anxiety in the moment.

If you are feeling anxious, listen closely and you will discover anxiety is talking. Broken down to its basic form it is fear. Anxiety primarily says, "It's not safe, it's not safe, it's not safe." But what is yours saying specifi-cally? If you're not in a situation that logically feels unsafe, I invite you to consider the idea of teaching the mind otherwise. A bit like our soothing a small child who is anxious, "But there's nothing to worry about," is likely ineffective, we can instead try to use a question.

Angels, how can I ease my anxiety?

Peace is the opposite of anxiety, so seek instead to have more peace. This is easier for the mind to create than getting rid of or managing something. Where is peace in your body now? Keep looking until you find it, then cultivate it. Make your body and your being a haven for peace. What is your life like when you are a haven for peace?

Work with MAGE to Help with Anxiety

A mage is a wise or learned person and is an aspect of Merlin, whom I'll talk about more in Chapter 28. Think of releasing the grip of your anxiety as tapping into your inner mage. Picture becoming a master of your emotions so that you can live your best life. Here are some of the things I have learned can help with anxiety, using the acronym MAGE (meaning, affirm, grounding, and exercise) to help you remember.

Meaning: Ask yourself, what will bring meaning to my day today? What do I want to create, on purpose? Two tools I use for this are to brainstorm ideas on a sheet of paper and to make to-do lists. My own list serves as an anchor that I can keep coming back to and which helps me to remember my intentions.

If you're feeling crippled by your anxiety, populate your list with easy things that you can most definitely do. Meaning can also mean reaching out to your community, to ask for help or for a chat or some company. Sometimes it's to help someone else. This is a great way to take the focus off us, which is something anxiety does, whipping us into a frenzy in our heads. Phone a friend, either to ask for help or to offer to help.

Some of us find it hard to ask for help. To say, *I'm anxious today and I could use some company. I find it hard, because I like to be the person who helps.* But this is a lesson—sometimes we all need other people, whether it's to go for tea with a friend or to ring the Samaritans. Reach out when you need to. We often give the very best advice to others that we could do with hearing ourselves. For example, if a friend tells you they are anxious, listen to the advice you give them. Make a note for yourself. Imagine a friend is asking your advice on what to do to help with their anxiety, and write down some ideas for "them," (i.e. you).

Affirm: If the opposite of unsafe is safe, think of affirmations you can say out loud and, in the mind, and even write out over and over if this helps.

- I Am Safe.

- I Am Strong.

- I Am Courage.

- I Am Wisdom.

You can also tap around the points, on page 141, or follow one of my YouTube *Angel EFT* videos for support and ideas. Think of as many affirmations as you can as you gently tap around the points while saying them, or else repeat your favourite one. This is you talking to the mind, telling it things are okay.

Grounding: When we experience anxiety, we have too much energy in and around the head as thoughts are spiralling. Breathe to come back into the body. Bring awareness to the soles of your feet. Imagine breathing in golden light that attracts many angels to you. Send golden energy roots deep into Mother Earth. Do some gardening if you can, or wash the dishes. I find looking at the vibrational scale grounding. Check in with where you are at and remember to ask the question, *How can I help myself to move up the scale one place just now?*

Exercise: Doing 20 minutes of cardiovascular exercise, if this is suitable for you, is a huge help for disrupting the grip of anxiety. If you have knee or leg problems, there are even cardio chair workouts you can find online. Yoga is fantastic. Putting on your favourite song and dancing. Going for a walk, or simply moving the body using exercises that cross over the midline, like cross-crawls, cook's hook-ups, or making figures-of-eight with your hands or your hips, can shift the energy and help you to step up out of anxiety. Exercise will help you to feel better.

Overwhelm is another subchapter of anxiety. Notice the times when you suffer from overwhelm. Sometimes it can feel justified if you have SO much to do. And then, what is the learning? Perhaps you have taken on too much. Or you could be learning the lesson of delegation or asking for help.

Angels, how do I raise myself up out of overwhelm?

Come back into your body. Organize thoughts by writing out
what needs to be done. Overwhelm is a fear of being unable to
act. Counter it by taking calm and confident action. Move your
body in flow. Dance.

When we get too much into "doing" mode we are stuck in the masculine energy. In order to feel good we need to balance our masculine and feminine energies (we all contain both; they are not determined by sex/gender). Here are some of the positive aspects of each:

Feminine:
- Emotional intelligence
- Creativity and receptivity
- Nurturing
- Intuition

Masculine:
- Logic and reason
- Discipline
- Protectiveness
- Stability and structure

You can balance yourself by receiving, taking time to rest, to withdraw, dream, journal, lie out in nature, swim . . .

Angels, how do I move into confidence and joy today?

Soften your body. Hands on belly. Hug yourself. Listen to high-
frequency sounds—talks or music or whatever lifts you to listen
to, to help raise up the thoughts.

Archangel Jophiel, how can I stop obsessional thoughts?

A mind that gets into repetitive obsessional thoughts and obsessions is seeking something. It gets confused by the lower vibrations that act like taking a bird off its course. Give it something else. Your biggest goal. Ask how may I serve? Picture how life looks when you are at your very highest vibrational state.

If another, unhelpful feeling accompanies the obsessional thought, associated with guilt, for example, or shame that you have those thoughts, create an affirmation to oppose it. For example, *There's something wrong with me that I think like this,* could become, simply:

I Am Light.

How Do I Get Rid of Anxiety?

I would rather think of releasing the grip than getting rid of anxiety, which seems a natural if uncomfortable human state. Our biggest downfall is to believe the thoughts that anxiety presents to us. Rather, try using MAGE to deal with anxiety, should it occur; it's very powerful. So that you are no longer afraid of it or dreading it. So that if it does arise, it's no big deal.

Ask yourself, what gifts does anxiety bring? For me, anxiety has been a great teacher. It shows me how strong and resilient I am in truth, and reminds me that I am a sensitive. If I wasn't, I wouldn't do the work that I do. It reminds me of all the skills I have learned.

Good Boundaries

Angels, how can I learn good boundaries?

When you ask this question you are already on the right path, for
you have become conscious of boundaries and where they have
failed. Pause before speaking. Hold still instead of nodding in
agreement when you don't agree. Your body will always tell you.
Come back to your body. When you come into your truth you
will stand and carry yourself accordingly.

Mina's Story

Mina told me she had terrible issues with boundaries, and she really
wanted to change, as she was constantly agreeing to things she didn't
truly feel comfortable with. She said, "People walk all over me." People
included her partner, her children, and her colleagues. Sometimes even
her friends. It was immediately clear from the way she sat that her throat
chakra was partially closed. I could see intuitively as she spoke that it
opened and closed as she spoke. Its message was that "it's not safe to
speak my truth."

It turned out that when Mina was a child she was regularly invali-
dated—mocked and emotionally punished through withdrawal of love
when she spoke her truth. She was expected to agree with everything
and not have her own opinion. She received the message loud and clear:
good girls are quiet and do as they're told. They weren't supposed to have
an opinion. This was passed down to her by her parents, who had also
received this message. It wasn't their fault, since it was modelled for them
too. Mina had the opportunity now to stop this pattern from passing
down to the next generation by resolving it. Remember that when you

break an unhealthy pattern that has passed down the ancestral line, this is great service to all of the family lineage.

Merging

As our sessions progressed Mina became more conscious of her body and what it was showing her. She even noticed that when she sat in the passenger seat of a car on a long journey she began to subtly lean into the driver's side, and took steps to correct her posture when she caught herself doing this. This was a perfect example of a merging of energy.

Unconsciously Mina had learned that to keep safe it's best to go along with the other person—even to blend into them energetically, almost like a chameleon. This made it easier to agree with them even if she didn't like what they were saying. In fact, one of the compliments she often received was that she was very empathetic and could understand anyone's point of view. While this is a gift, in her case it sometimes slipped down the vibrational scale, leading to her not being true to herself.

Saying No to Say Yes

Mina became more and more aware of instances where she wasn't speaking her truth, and at times she felt as though she might give up, worrying that she'd never change. Yet she did practise new ways and was making progress. She learned how to say no. At first, she was terrified of losing people's approval, or of not being loved. And this very fear sometimes seemed to manifest just that. Yet as she got better at it, her relationships improved. She learned to own her feelings and express them when others made her uncomfortable. She thought about it like this: sometimes I need to say no to others in order to say yes to me.

Tadasana

Mina started going to yoga, which she told me helped her to be in her body even more. Best of all she loved mountain pose, and she said the Sanskrit name, tadasana, always made her smile as it reminded her of her telling herself, *Ta-da! Here I am. This is who I am. I'm not hiding any more.* Tadasana is a great pose for many reasons, but superb for being fully present in your body. And it's so simple—as long as you can stand, you can do it. You can even do it while in the queue at the supermarket.

And Mina is still empathetic, although she no longer lets anyone walk over her. If any extra-hard boundary tests come her way (as they do from time to time), she is grateful. Because if the old behaviour surfaces, of being afraid to stand up for herself, she immediately spots it and learns from it.

When Mina corrected boundaries in her life, things began to improve for her on many other levels, like a positive domino effect. This shows how, when one aspect of our life is out of balance, it affects the whole, and so does correcting it.

Archangel Michael, how can I unblock my throat chakra?

Sing, say mantras and affirmations, and use sounds. Make friends
with your voice and your throat. Words are so important.
What are you saying each day? Speak words with intention. Your
throat chakra governs communication. It is also connected to
your creativity. Writers and artists need a clear throat chakra
to create their art.

Unblocking Your Throat Chakra

1. Place the palm of one hand on your throat chakra, or throat area. How does it feel in there? The palm chakras in your hand are opening and awakening, and they are making a connection—a communication—with your throat chakra. Close your eyes and be open to receiving information about this area. Write down any insights.

2. Now, visualize Archangel Michael filling your throat chakra with light. At first, the light may show you any blocks that exist there. They may appear like shapes, colours, feelings, or as symbols. You may even see people in there, or conversations. Just be open to what shows up.

3. Now that you have acknowledged any limitations, Archangel Michael fills your throat chakra with his powerful deep blue light. It also contains the glowing silver-gold light of his sword, which can burn up and transmute any blocks that you give permission to release now.

Be open to the learning that comes, for then the next time the situation arises you will know what to do and have a choice of whether to go with the new way or repeat the old. If you repeat the old, you can reflect on it and be ready for the next time. Ask yourself, *What might I say or do differently?*

If there is a lesson that keeps showing up and you find it difficult to break the old pattern, get used to saying the things that you've found hard to say. Say them to yourself in the mirror, or when you're alone, as though you are an actor rehearsing their lines. Get used to these words in your mouth. See yourself in the mirror using the facial expression and body posture that best goes with them. With practice, you will become more comfortable, and the new response will become more natural.

Speak as though you expect the other person to see your point of view. When we speak from the heart in a genuine way, it matters less if we are making a big request of the other person. They are free to respond how they wish. If we cower when we speak, or use a whining or complaining tone, for example, we appear as though we don't expect the other person to agree or help us.

Your Shining Sun—Solar Plexus

Watch how you are standing or sitting to get a feeling for your solar plexus. If you caught yourself slouching, for example, you might be feeling disempowered. Come back into your power by adjusting your posture. Spine straight, shoulders back, and deep full breath tells the solar plexus that it is full of light and powerful.

Archangel Uriel, how can I strengthen my solar plexus chakra?

Place your hands on your solar plexus chakra, which is a solar sun within your being. Feel its light and give it permission to expand. As you do, it cleanses itself naturally, and the solar light of your solar plexus stretches out far and wide. See it reaching faraway places. Send it through time to yourself at times when you felt less powerful. Empower these past versions of yourself and they too usher in strength for the now.

There are yoga poses (*asanas*) that you can use specifically to strengthen your solar plexus chakra, such as cobra or bow pose. Or hold an iron pyrite or any of the crystals associated with this chakra to it and breathe the energy of the crystal in. To work with a crystal, cleanse it first; you can do this by asking the angels to cleanse it for you, or by placing them out in nature—check if your crystal is affected by water, though. Because the solar plexus is like the sun, it is at your centre. Imagine the centre of your being as a huge great golden sun. Then shine your rays out.

Grounding

It is easier to have good boundaries when we are grounded. Imagine someone who is ungrounded. This looks like, energetically, their feet don't quite touch the ground. Or else they are easily swayed or knocked off balance, since they are not quite in their body. It is easy for them to be pushed around. When you are grounded you are solid and steady in your aura. You belong here on Earth and believe in yourself. Work with the lower chakras, especially the root or base chakra, to be grounded.

Archangel Gabriel, how can I strengthen my root chakra?

Send your energy down into the planet. If you have been habitually living in your head and daydreaming, bring your focus into the present, into your body, into the Earth below your feet. Know where you are, dear one. You chose this Earth and, yes, you belong here just now. So, own it.

Mountain pose, child's pose, and thunderbolt pose are some yoga *asanas* to help with grounding and activating the base chakra. If you've been ungrounded for a long time, you will need to keep coming back to this lesson. When you are ungrounded, you are vulnerable to not having good boundaries, as well as to other challenges. So it's worth mastering this important lesson. Ask the question every day for as long as you need to.

Less Stress, More Peace

Angels, how can I be less stressed?

Ask that one again.

Okay. Angels, how can I feel peace and confidence right now?

Slow down. Move with ease and grace like you are an angel.

This made me laugh, being asked to ask it again—to rephrase the question. I know precisely why the angels told me that: because the mind has an easier time creating something than it does getting rid of or having less of something. We must work with the mind when we want to change our state. The idea of walking as though I'm an angel both amused and fascinated me. If I were in a drama class and was asked to walk like an angel, I think I would walk in a very calm, "floaty" way. The opposite of pounding around in a stressed way.

Walking like an Angel

1. Begin by standing straight, balanced on both feet as equally as you can, palms facing outward, with a sense of being deeply connected to the Earth and steady.

2. Now close your eyes or soften your gaze. Feel yourself being filled with golden light coming down through the higher chakras and in through the crown. Flowing all the way down the body and through the feet into the Earth below.

3. Imagine that you are becoming an angel. Feel the tingling at your shoulder blades as your wings of light start to emerge and unfurl. Take some calming breaths as they do. How far out do they span?

4. Slowly, when you feel ready, open your eyes and see the world through your angel eyes.

5. Gently begin to move, mindfully and as though your body is made purely of light. Walk around, either where you are, or outside might be even nicer. Allow your facial muscles to soften, your jaw, and your shoulders.

The Magic of Time Expansion

Slowing down to combat stress can sound counter-intuitive. Usually when we're stressed the idea of slowing down appears preposterous because we feel there's already not enough time and too much to do. Yet we create this sense of not having enough time, which then often manifests, through our stressed thoughts. Practising slowing down doesn't mean doing nothing, but rather doing things in a calm and focused manner with purpose.

Be open to the possibility that with your thoughts you can "expand" your experience of time. For example, you might like to use the affirmation, "I have plenty of time to do all that I need." If your inner talk is always about not having enough time, you can learn to retrain this by using affirmations and reaching for higher thought.

If you hear others saying, "Time goes quickly, already it's (insert month/season, etc.)!," you don't need to agree with that. To do so is to accept it into your reality. Immerse yourself in the present. What are you noticing right now? What is there in this moment? The above exercise on walking like an angel can help with this.

Finding the Origin to Uncover Solutions

Try asking the angels what things have typically stressed you out up to now, and then what you might do about each of them. Are they all unavoidable and inescapable? You likely have the power to change some of these things at least. To alter the script and the narrative of what you say to yourself.

Sadiq was overwhelmed trying to keep his home tidy and didn't get much help from his children. He asked the angels the following question, and this is what he received:

Angels, how do I get more help with the home?

Ask calmly and be specific. Write it out visually for your children.
Expect that help. If you ask and are exasperated or irritated, this
gives them the message that you don't expect them to help.

Sadiq got interesting results when he changed his approach, and he went on to apply this same advice in his job. Things improved there as well, and he received more help with tasks he'd been struggling alone with.

I loved the reminder that Sadiq was given, of expecting to receive when we ask for something. It's so true that, if we doubt the other person will help or do the thing, we are giving that message in our body language, in our tone of voice, and also saying it loud and clear to the universe. Think of times someone else has asked you to do something in this doubtful way. Did them sounding cross or disbelieving make you want to do it? Or was it a bit contagious, making you doubt you'd do it either?

Other Questions to Help Create a More Peaceful Day

Angels, how best can I navigate an amazing day today?

Soften. Focus on how you'd like to feel later today. As you are
getting ready for bed and reflecting on the day, what things
would you like to have happened or be in place that you can do?
What things can you create today that facilitate that?

Angels, how can I feel more peace in my life in general?

Look at how you are putting yourself forward in life. Are you
rushing and pushing all the time? Do you need to come into
your feminine energy more? Receive. Rest. Invite peace and make

your body and mind a place peace likes to be. Tap on the word peace. Call upon the angels of peace. Make peace your project. The inner reflects the outer. When you create peace so you will see it around you.

Rushing and Pushing and the "B" Word

There can be an addictiveness to the state of always rushing and pushing, and it's encouraged in many cultures. Pushing is pushing against something. When we are in flow, we glide through doors that open beautifully for us. When we're rushing and pushing, life can feel like an uphill struggle, but hard to step off.

The "b" word is busy. Say the phrase now: "I'm busy." Try out different tones of voice and facial expressions. Be playful. How does it make you feel? When others say it to you, how does that feel? The word busy is full of variety. On the one hand, it can feel good to be busy. It might mean productive. Useful. Important. In the world of the self-employed, it can be equated to successful. It can also become a word that keeps others at bay. If you are busy, you are unavailable.

Constantly busy people seem to hold their breath and not fill their lungs properly, as though there isn't time even for that. They're always in a hurry and can exhibit a sense of martyrdom, as though life has forced this state upon them. But has it? If this sounds familiar to you, ask yourself, *What is my role in this? If I want to change, what steps am I willing to take?* Think of what questions you might ask the angels to help change this situation.

In EFT, we sometimes ask, what are the gains of having this problem? For the busy rusher-pusher aspect, it could be a sense of duty. For example, the high-powered executive is expected to be on the go all the time, finger on the pulse, not resting and taking time for her self-care. The dutiful mother icon who feels she must not rest but be constantly doing and wouldn't dream of taking a day for herself. The self-employed tradesman who cannot take a day off.

This behaviour is typically masculine, "doing" all the time and not being able to receive or to be. Feminine energy is soft and receptive. Creatives need to be in their feminine energy to allow ideas to flow in. They also need masculine energy to push the idea forward and bring it into the world. A balance of the two is the perfect combination.

We're all connected, and this is why self-care is not selfish. This is for those of you who find self-care difficult. Or see it as a luxury you're not quite sure what to do with. If you've been told you need to reduce stress to be healthy, or to overcome dis-ease, you might feel highly motivated. Think of peace, or another, similar word, such as calm, flow, love, unity, light, ease, relax. A friend I met when I was training in EFT told me he uses the name of a beautiful lake he loves. You might choose your favourite colour, or an archangel you like to work with.

I encourage clients, and myself, to be the listener to the thoughts that come up. To understand what we are saying to ourselves, about ourselves, about the world, and about our lives. Those thoughts that reoccur over and over have etched a path, and, if they are not helpful thoughts, we have the choice and ability to follow new ones. Listen to your thoughts so you can change and master them.

Golden Thoughts Exercise

1. Light a candle and take some calming breaths.

2. Imagine a golden thought that you would like to be a part of your reality; e.g., an affirmation. It begins as a tiny flicker in your mind.

3. What is this thought? Is it a plan? An intention? A gratitude? Notice as the thought begins to expand and glow what it is like.

4. See a host of angels energizing the thought, expanding it with light.

5. Envision the thought lighting the way ahead of you and receive energy and enthusiasm from it.

6. Notice how the thought makes your body feel.

Wonderful Sleep

Sleep restores our mind, body, and spirit. Without a good night's sleep, we're not at our best, and so of course the angels want to help us with this. If you ask them, they may drop ideas into your mind during the day about how to improve your sleep. Brainstorm your ideas and make a plan. Are you consuming too many stimulants? Are you bringing your phone/device to bed with you and using it in the night when you can't sleep, thus creating a learned behaviour and stimulating the brain when you're trying to get it to slow down?

Find what feels best to you. If you have your phone there for the alarm, you could either leave it on flight mode or get an old-fashioned alarm clock instead. If you take alcohol, notice how it affects your sleep. Contrary to the old belief that alcohol helps sleep, it reduces the quality of sleep and has tricky energies that could affect your sense of peace and well-being. Ask the angels what you need to know.

I like the advice given by Mel Robbins in her book *The 5-Second Rule*. Mel says she leaves her phone in the bathroom and doesn't allow herself to look at it until she's up and has completed all her important routines. Before she lets the world come crashing in, distracting her with what she describes as everybody else's stuff. This is a superb productivity tip but also keeps you in your own authentic energy. If you're in bed reading emails or the news or checking social media, you're letting all that "stuff" of other people into your sacred resting space.

Angels, how can I get back to sleep?

You are in a peaceful, empty room now. What is the room like?
How high is the ceiling? Those people you've been thinking
about are there with you, but it's time to sleep. So let them go

now and watch them leaving the room, one by one. Say goodbye and let them go with love. You are in the perfect space for sleep and it's just you.

I found when I did this I became sleepier. The people and situations I was thinking about in the middle of the night had been permitted to go, so there was nothing to sort out. You might like to try this exercise. But ask your angels too and be open to receiving the advice perfect for you.

Your Sacred Sleeping Space

Whether you sleep alone or with a partner, and/or child or pet, you can focus on making your sleep space a sacred place. Tune in to your sleep space now. Is the bed made? Does it have fresh, clean sheets? There's no need to over-wash your bedding, as to do so is uneconomical, wasting lots of water and power, but having at least a regularly cleaned pillowcase makes it a more inviting space. Open the windows in the morning to let in the fresh air, and set the intention as you do of releasing the thoughts and energies of the night. Some people find sprinkling a drop of lavender oil on their pillow helpful for sleep, but know that too much lavender acts as a stimulant. Synthetic sleep sprays can affect sensitive people, but you can make your own, like this one:

Make Your Own Angelic Sleep Spray
UTENSILS

1. A blue glass spray bottle or other suitable clean spray bottle free from odours.

2. Water (I use filtered or cooled boiled; some people like to use distilled water).

3. A large bowl for the water. I use a glass casserole dish with a lid.

4. A small bowl or glass, if you are using crystals and don't want them to be directly in the water (some crystals will spoil if you put them in water, especially those with names ending in -ite).

5. Something to cover the bowl(s) if you don't have a glass lid.

6. Crystals or gemstones suitable for sleep. Amethyst, clear quartz, selenite, moonstone, are known to help you sleep, and I also like rose quartz.

7. A candle.

8. A funnel or small jug and a ladle.

9. Some people like to add a little organic alcohol to help preserve their spray.

10. And, if you would like, a few drops of essential oils that you like the fragrance of and which are suitable for sleep; lavender, Roman chamomile, sandalwood, and ylang-ylang are all popular.

METHOD

11. Light a candle. Energetically clear yourself, the necessary utensils, and the space by calling in Archangel Michael and asking him to cleanse the space and your aura in readiness.

12. Prepare your large bowl of distilled or filtered water.

13. For crystals kept separate, add a smaller bowl or glass (whose inside stays dry) into the larger bowl.

14. Invoke the dusky pink dragons of Andromeda and ask them to pour transcendent love into your sleep spray and balance your chakras while you sleep and rest. Invoke Archangel Jophiel to help your mind to release thoughts and rest.

15. Invoke the crystal devas of your chosen crystals, or, if you don't have any, tune in to the energy of the moonstone in the planet and ask her to pour her light into your spray for peaceful sleep. Ask them all to please put their love, light, frequency, and energy for peace in the water and anchor it there. Hold the crystals and make a connection, and ask for their assistance in helping you to sleep well and easily.

16. Be open to any messages or insights that you receive.

17. Remember to thank all the beings for their blessings.

18. Place your crystals in the water, or in the bowl/glass. Cover the bowl(s) and leave for several hours or overnight. You can place the bowl in both the sun and the moonlight to add

both masculine and feminine energies, either outside or on a windowsill.

19. Light a candle and thank the angels, dragons, masters, and crystals. Using the ladle and funnel (or a little jug), add the blessed and energized water into the spray bottle. This is the time to add organic alcohol if you are using it, then your essential oils, and gently shake it until everything has mixed well.

20. Your spray is ready. I add a label so I can remember what I used to make the spray and what it's for.

Every time you apply this spray to your sleep space, you add the energy of peace, love, and relaxation and any other intentions you have added to your spray.

Night Travellers and Warriors

I hear many lightworkers say that they suspect they leave their bodies at night and are off in other dimensions and galaxies helping people and situations. I agree that this is totally possible. When I was in my teens a family friend was staying over one night. She was upset at the time and didn't sleep well. In the morning, she thanked me for coming into the room and comforting her in the night. I don't have any history of sleep-walking and am fairly sure I didn't go into her room. I wondered if it was my spirit that did this, and this is what she experienced.

If you are one of these night travellers, ask your angels to guide you to places that your spirit is well equipped for. Ask them to protect you and heal you. Angel wisdom is that we are here to serve but not to become slaves or martyrs. This comes from a lower dimension and is another lesson for some of us to master.

Cutting Cords for a Good Night's Sleep

I have a free visualization for cutting cords with Archangel Michael available on my website if you need some guidance in doing this. If you're new to cord-cutting, try listening to it each evening for a week and see how differently you feel. For those of you who are used to cutting cords, are you still remembering to do it? I need to remind myself sometimes too. A good prompt to remember to cut your cords is if you're feeling drained and can't imagine why. If you ask, the angels will show you why you are feeling drained and help you to cut any cords that are responsible. Some people even release pain this way also.

Worrying About Tomorrow?

If you're not sleeping because you're worried about the following day and all you need to do, sometimes writing things down can help. It eases the mind to get those things down on paper. Sometimes we can't sleep because we have so many things we are trying to remember for the day ahead, and writing them down can unburden your mind of trying not to forget them.

Ask the angels, *How can I feel calm about tomorrow?* See them taking some of those things you've been carrying for you so you don't have such a heavy load.

Johanna was worried about a family member who was going through a big challenge. It affected her sleep, and she was waking in the night, totally preoccupied. Her angel guidance was to write down a simple, "Angels, please help Gareth," and each night before bed to place this message on her angel altar under a crystal. She would choose an angel card for him, and then let it go. She told herself she was handing the situation over to the angels, and she began to sleep through the night again. If she woke, she remembered that she had done what she could for now and was able to drop off again. She liked to write the message on a fresh piece of paper each night and let the old one go in the morning.

Breathing for Sleep

There are certain *pranayamas* (yogic breathing techniques) that help sleep, such as alternate nostril breathing. But if you are in bed already and don't want to sit up, imagine breathing in a lovely relaxing colour. As you breathe in, this beautiful colour lights up all the cells in your body and helps them to release any toxins, anything that's been worrying them. Imagine each cell has a consciousness of its own and is relaxing now.

Brainstorming for Sleep

A daytime activity is to brainstorm your ideas on how to improve your sleep. What are all the things you can think of to improve your sleep now? Write down your ideas. If you are willing to make those changes, even one at a time if there are many changes to make, your sleep should improve. And of course, ask, *Angels, is there anything else I need to know about how to improve my sleep?*

PART FOUR

CARING FOR OTHERS

15

Healing the Empath

Many lightworkers are also sensitive beings who care for others, known as empaths. They feel things so deeply that at times it is as though there is no outer edge to their aura, or that they are "without skin." They sense an argument in a room when there is nobody in there any more. They feel spirits whose essence hangs around buildings. They receive someone else's emotions (particularly painful ones) as though they are their own, and sometimes can't even tell that they are not their own. These sensitives are compassionate folks who like to heal others either in the usual ways, or without speaking or appearing to do anything. Kind, smiling people who may unwittingly wear a worried frown sometimes, and who are generally nice to meet.

You may be an empath if:

- People frequently tell you their problems and lean on you for emotional support.

- You are known for being caring.

- You intuitively sense how another person (or animal or any sentient being) is feeling.

- You feel the pain of others' suffering, including the natural world, and this has overwhelmed you at times.

- Being in nature makes you feel better and you have a heightened awareness of this.

- You sometimes feel entities in buildings.

- You feel energy from crystals.

- You find being in crowds challenging.

- You would describe yourself as sensitive.

- You sometimes urgently need time alone.

- You remember a person less for how they look and more for how they "felt," energetically, to you.

If this resonates with you, I invite you to consider for a moment that the empath is just a part of you and not all of you. We have many parts, and overidentifying with any of them can lead to imbalance through labelling, where we "live up to the description," instead of being the radiant, multidimensional beings that we are.

For the empath part of you, perhaps it began in your youngest of years, trying to heal those in the family around you. Maybe even in the womb as you felt your mother's emotions. Or at school. Seeing energies. Getting to work and using your powers to lighten the mood of others with your smiles and kindness and fun. Your healing touch. You felt the pain of animals deeply, as well as that of people.

This sensitive part of you is precious. The school we are on (Earth) has harsh lessons and dense energies and now it is time for some healing for your inner empath. As I write this, the sun is rising and the yellow light and that of a rainbow comes through the trees. I know it is telling me about the solar plexus and Uriel's fifth-dimensional rainbow light.

The Maladaptive Empath

The hurt empath can develop maladaptive behaviours. Addictions are an attempt to numb out pain and discomfort, or fill them up when they feel empty. This is a third-dimensional attempt to manage, and, although common, the time to heal it is now. It's time for each of us to step up and be who we came here to be. Your light is important. Get the help you need so you can align with your mission. Once you do (you may be delighted to know) you will have the capability to truly help others with the same issue, should you desire it.

Archangel Uriel, how can I heal my inner empath?

We are surrounding your inner child now and bringing them
the light that they need to heal. Call forward the Rainbow Fire
to wash the solar plexus. Ask it to remove all debris and all that
is not serving you. Give permission for what you have held and
carried for others to be released. Send an angel to anyone you
have been consciously carrying, knowing that you need not carry
them now. Put them down. They are looked after.

Visualize your inner child dancing in light. Playing and having fun, surrounded by angels. Archangel Uriel is pouring golden rainbow light into
your solar plexus chakra now. This upgrades any third-dimensional com-
ponents to the fifth dimension, where we do not need to absorb the pain
of others any more.

Diana Cooper says that instead, the fifth-dimensional solar plexus
chakra reaches for wisdom. Herein our solar plexus chakra is evolved and
radiates a light that naturally helps others to feel safe, without the need
to absorb anything from them as the spongelike third-dimensional solar
plexus chakra did.

If you have a specific memory of taking on someone else's pain that
sticks out, work with this now if it feels okay. And if not, make a note of
it and get support to work on it. Perhaps there are so many instances that
you are not aware of any particular one.

Shields and Protection

Protect yourself, your energy, and your aura regularly. I have worked with
all of the following ways of protection and found each of them helpful
in their own way.

- The Violet Flame

- Archangel Michael's deep blue light and/or sword of light

- The Rainbow Fire of Source (see page 206)

- The Gold Ray of Christ

- The Gold, Silver, and Violet Flame

- The Lilac Fire of Source

- Archangel Metatron's Cloak and/or Metatron's Cube

- Mother Mary's Aquamarine Cloak

- The Cosmic Diamond Violet Flame

- Sanat Kumara's Sunshine Aqua Light (see page 93).

If you feel you have absorbed something that doesn't belong, cleanse it away by radiating brighter. Using the "I Am" in front of any of the suggestions above is effective. For example: "I Am the Gold Ray of Christ." Or, "I now invoke the Lilac Fire of Source for my total protection."

Archangel Michael's Deep Blue Dragons

Call upon Archangel Michael's deep blue dragons to protect and clear the way. They will work to protect not just your aura and space but up to a mile radius all around you. Send them deep into the Earth to clear the land below your feet. Send them around buildings. To your workplace. To people. Ask them to surround you if you are facing someone who presses your buttons.

Journal of the Empath

Healing your inner empath may be one of your major soul lessons and you may need to come back to it. If this is the case, you could start to journal for the inner empath for 21 days. See how you evolve over this time. Use the visualization overleaf at the end of each day to cleanse your energy before you go to bed. Jot down any insights that you receive. Over time you will get stronger at managing this. If you have completed the 21 days and it crops up again later, you will have a deeper insight the next time and be able to correct and improve your energy management.

Gold, Silver, and Violet Flame Dragons Visualization

1. Close your eyes and see three beautiful gold, silver, and violet flame dragons approaching you.

2. One sits in front of you, one behind you, and the other one hovers above you.

3. When you are ready, ask the dragons to breathe their loving gold, silver, and violet flame over you.

4. The dragon above begins, and the flame comes down through your fifth-dimensional chakra column: the stellar gateway chakra, the soul star, the causal, the crown, the third eye, the throat, the heart, the solar plexus, the navel, the sacral, the base, the earth star chakra.

5. Each chakra now blazes with this flame that is clearing away any debris, blazing it into harmless energy, and turning up the volume of your light.

6. Know that you are a vibrant being of light and you do not need to carry anything that doesn't belong to you. This goes even for those closest to you, who will benefit more greatly from your support when you do not attempt to carry things for them. Be instead a loving, compassionate witness who shines light on everything and everyone.

7. The dragons behind and in front of you are now breathing their fire over you and it is making a huge ball of light around you. This is being activated for today, and you can ask them to refresh it daily for as long as you need. It serves to prevent you from absorbing the pain of others, and to help you to learn the lesson of the empath, which is to be a blazing light and hold your integrity.

8. Feel this light around you and infusing your being. You are so loved and completely held by the dragons. Your whole aura has taken on the colours gold, silver, and violet. You are a blazing light who has come to serve and to enjoy your life.

9. Ask these three dragons their names and be open to receiving them.

10. Write them down and know to call on these dragons and work with them. They are there for you whenever you need them.

11. Now, if there is anyone or anything you have been worrying about, send a host of new gold, silver, and violet flame dragons to the person or situation. See them going straight there and helping with their blazing light. Give yourself permission to detach with love, so you are no longer tethered.

12. Thank the dragons and bring your awareness fully into your body and the place you started.

Helping Others

How do I help someone else?

Know that you can help someone else by raising your frequency
when you think about them. See them bathed in light, see them
in their divine perfection.

I loved hearing this. It's so true. A little bit like when someone says, "You poor thing," or "Isn't that awful, how can they cope with something like that," or any such pitying phrases about someone—this is not helpful. Instead, say, "I really admire her courage." Or, "His tenacity really inspires me," and so on. Seeing the strengths in someone helps to uncover those strengths for them. Avoid getting into fear when you think of other people. It's natural when something tragic or harrowing happens to someone to feel sorry for them, but learn to choose your thoughts and words with care to send them the best energy. And above all, send them angels.

Sending Angels to Someone Else

One of my most popular blogs and videos is about sending angels to other people. Can the angels help someone else when they don't ask, but we ask for them? And if the person doesn't even believe in angels? When we ask the angels to help someone else, we bring in light. It's important to be able to do this and then let go. It can be challenging, especially if you feel very invested in helping that person. But it's a kindness to them to ask and then let go. It doesn't mean you stop caring or wondering about them, but when you've already asked, you can then release it.

Respecting Someone's Right to Choose

The other person has their own soul journey and challenges. They also have the absolute right not to be helped, to make poor choices, and even to cause harm to themselves. We can't interfere with that and nor can the angels. But asking the angels creates a bridge of light whereupon that person has help, should they choose to reach for it. And for some, that bridge will make the difference.

So it is always worth asking. If you are feeling helpless about someone else, it is one positive action you can take that doesn't fall into rescuing/enabling or other unhelpful patterns.

How Can I Best Help Someone Who Is Gravely Ill?

Similarly to the above, first understand that not only does someone have the right to be terminally ill or addicted/self-destructive etc., but that we each have a soul contract to incarnate for a certain length of time. Some of us will die young, but not before our time, since we agreed on this before we incarnated. The reason might be one we can't understand while we are here in our earth bodies.

Still, I have found that, by using Angel EFT, I can do something positive when someone is gravely ill. I'll never know for sure if it helped because it's not measurable, but it always feels good and lightens up my thoughts, so I can help by visualizing that person making a full recovery. Worrying about someone is a typical human emotion, but it's much more helpful to hold the vision of that person as well and happy. You can proxy tap for someone else. It's really very simple. Even tapping around the points and saying the person's name can be helpful.

Example phrases to use while tapping on the points:

- Angels, thank you for the perfect healing of . . .
- Angels helping . . .

- Angels are surrounding . . . and are working through her medical team.

- Archangel Raphael is with . . . for their highest good.

- Angel healing for . . .

- Healing angels are helping . . . to visualize his full recovery. And so it is.

What If the Person Doesn't Believe in Angels?

It doesn't matter if that person doesn't believe. We each have a guardian angel who stays with us throughout our lives, no matter whether we ever acknowledge them. Our guardian angel doesn't interfere in our lives if we never ask for their help. Unless there is a life-or-death situation, and only then can they step in uninvited—if it's not our time to die.

In the summer of 1999, I fell off a building onto a roof of a petrol station three floors below—more than ten metres. Although I had trained in Reiki, I didn't believe in angels at this time, but I now understand that my angel stepped in and softened my fall. I broke both femurs and patellae but suffered no spine or head injury. In theatre having complex emergency surgery, I went into renal failure because of the shock and the medics thought I wasn't going to make it. This is the phone call my parents received: "Your daughter has been in a serious accident and I'm afraid we're losing her."

But then things suddenly turned around. When I woke in ICU and saw the faces of my mum and dad, I felt as though I was a wise being, and their parent instead. I can only describe it as a sort of heavenly moment. It was like I'd come back from somewhere spectacular and had to comfort these worried-looking Earthlings.

Heroes and Rescuers—a Word of Caution

If you notice a tendency in yourself to want to rescue others, be mindful of this and reach out for your own help when needed. It's good service to help others, but putting everyone else before yourself is unbalanced. Sometimes we can best assist others by demonstrating healthy ways in our own lives, rather than doing things for them and trying to learn their lessons for them. It's a trap that caring folks can fall into and it will drain their energy – yet it is a super learning opportunity when they understand what's happening.

How to recognize if you've become a hero or rescuer. You:

- Worry a lot about a person (or people).

- Rally around doing things for others that really they could do themselves but aren't doing, or aren't doing quickly enough.

- Feel responsible more than is appropriate.

- Spend a lot of time in your head thinking about how you might help them even more—or solve problems for them.

- Neglect other things in your life because of all the energy you're putting into this person.

- Feel like they are almost part of your energy field.

This is a two-way street, and the other person may attract this kind of rescuing. They may have had a series of rescuers rallying around them before. And yet you can only do something about your role in it. The lesson is to release your grip, and possibly to let go. To let them be.

It's possible to get obsessed or unhealthily attached to helping someone else, and, if this is the case for you, you will know it and be able to decide when you are ready to address it. The sooner the better for both you and the other party, since this kind of obsession is not helpful or empowering and rests in the lower vibrations on the scale.

We can't fix people, they can only "fix" themselves. But personally, I don't like the notion that anyone is broken in the first place. Rather that they may have fallen into unhelpful ways. At all times, unless they are at death's door and have committed to dying, they have the potential to change if they so choose. To make better choices. And if they are dying, often they still have some choices. This is because, in the space of a split second, we can raise our consciousness.

Break an Unhealthy Attachment of Being a Hero or Rescuer

If those things resonated with you and you recognize an unhealthy attachment in trying to help someone, you can detach from this with love whenever you are ready. Ask Archangel Michael to dissolve the cords you have formed with them, and be willing to let this be done.

Reach out for help if you need it; you don't have to do it alone. This might be a pattern you have had for a long time or something that has been passed down from an ancestor. If you resolve the issue, you are helping future generations too by doing so, and the person concerned will feel freer.

Visualization to Release Someone

1. Feel your feet firmly on the ground. Call in Archangel Michael, Archangel Metatron, and Archangel Raphael.

2. See them surrounding you with light. Relax as their light weaves and circles around you, and notice any colours.

3. Ask Archangel Metatron to run his sacred geometrical cube (see page 82) through your chakra system, starting at the stellar gateway, down through the soul star, causal, crown, third eye, throat, heart, solar plexus, navel, sacral, base, and earth star, and note the feelings of each as it goes through. There may be messages for you.

4. Ask Archangel Raphael to bring an image of the other person that you have been helping. See them before you. Notice how they look when accompanied by the angels. Ask Archangel Raphael, "What insights do I need in this situation?"

5. See the person's higher self above them, and their own guardian angel. Do they have a message for you?

6. Archangel Michael is stepping forward and he illuminates cords that have formed between you and this person. Notice where in the body you see them. Archangel Michael hands you a small dagger made of crystal light and invites you to cut the cords, one by one. As you do, see each one loosening and releasing from the root and any remaining roots or pieces dissolving completely into divine light. The entire cord dissolves into the light so no roots are left in the other person either. See if you can cut all of them. If you feel you can't, repeat this again, the next day and for as many days as you need until all the cords are cut. This doesn't release love for the person; rather it frees them up from lower-frequency attachment.

7. Know that you are free. Thank the angels and archangels and release the other person with kindness. See them walking on their own path with confidence and strength, surrounded by light.

17

World Events and the Collective Consciousness

Angels, how do I keep my energy clear in the face of all that's going on in the world?

Come from drama and back into yourself. You chose to come here, it is the perfect school for you. You are exactly where you are meant to be and have the precise tools with which to manage. Your wisdom is not outside of yourself. Imagine that you are standing in a storm, that whirlpools of air are rushing around you. The elements are pushing against over and around you. Rain, wind, and such. You are strong and steady. Stand where you are. Feel your connection to Mother Earth who always loves you and is glad you are here on her planet. Detox from stories and fear clouds. Now see the storm moving on and feel sunlight.

One of the biggest challenges people face today is to stay pure and strong in your energy and your mindset and not get pulled around by fear and drama.

The News

The news is designed to grab our attention and this is done with shocking, adrenaline-inducing headlines that make us physically gasp or hold our breath. The music that accompanies the news can even sound apocalyptic. Often news stories are told in such a way that the listener/viewer is left feeling helpless. I seldom see any suggestions on the news as to how I can help a situation. Knowing what I know, I understand I can send angels, dragons, and other high-frequency helpers to the situation. Light a candle. Create a special meditation.

I want to acknowledge that I'm hugely grateful to the courageous journalists who risk their lives to uncover things that are otherwise hidden and go on behind closed doors. The work they do is phenomenal and has led to positive change and help being available. There are very important lightworkers in these roles, especially indigos and other light warriors.

Also, the news can show us important things, and keep us in the loop. But finding your boundaries within this is helpful. For many, listening to the headlines every day, and allowing news notifications on our phone, would be totally overwhelming. See what feels right for you and go with that. Listen/watch/read while standing in your power—in your own authentic energy.

Come Back Within

If you like to keep abreast of world events and current affairs, learn how to master your energy when you do so. Know that the headlines are written in an emotive, energy-grabbing way, so you can view them in context and not get pulled off-centre.

Protecting Yourself with Light

1. Take a breath and call your dragons to surround you. The fire dragons will purify your energy by breathing their bright fires in and around you, burning up anything that is less than love and dissolving it into light.

2. Ask Archangel Michael to surround you in his protective shielding blue orb so that nothing can get in that doesn't belong to you.

3. Focus on raising your frequency very high and opening your heart so that your heart's light touches your eyes and ears and you see things through the eyes of love.

4. Connect with your navel chakra, around the belly button and just above. This is your oneness chakra and sees beyond the us and them, the right and wrong, the good and evil. Through this chakra's wisdom you can feel the oneness of us all.

5. Ask Archangel Uriel to fill your solar plexus chakra to overflow with golden rainbow light that expands far out around you like a shimmering sun.

6. Imagine a golden grid of light that connects everybody on the planet from heart to heart.

7. Know that anyone behaving badly is still held within the non-judgemental light of the grid and is being whispered to by angels to wake up. See them waking up and realizing their divine potential.

Now, when you are reading, listening to, or looking at the news, you should feel strong and filled with light. How does it make you feel? What comes next, after you've watched it?

If you feel moved to help a situation you've learned about, try the following visualization:

Visualization to Help a Situation Remotely

1. Relax into your chair or stand barefoot on the Earth. Connect with your feet and imagine sending down energy roots to the heart of loving Mother Earth. She sends you love and welcome.

2. See the angels pouring light down over you and through you. Imagine the chakras waking up and expanding as they fill with light.

3. See your heart expanding especially, and your solar plexus.

4. Archangel Chamuel is filling your heart with brilliant white light with every colour within it.

5. Archangel Uriel is filling your solar plexus with golden wisdom.

6. Archangel Michael is protecting you with his deep blue light and clearing the throat chakra to help you speak your highest wisdom.

7. Call to mind the situation or images you've seen or heard about.

8. Ask the dragons to go to the situation now. The dragons can delve deep into any darkness to clear it. Let them do their work.

9. As the frequency rises, angels come in. They are spreading golden light everywhere.

10. Detach with love, thanking the wise beings who have helped and will continue to help if appropriate. Come fully back into your body.

11. Think of something you love and smile.

What Can I Do to Serve?

There is lots we can do to help. By meditating, sending light, and raising your frequency generally, you help the world. By tensing your body and feeling fearful and sad you are adding to a cloud of fear that has been perpetuated right through the Piscean age and is what we are overcoming in the new Aquarian age. In the new Golden age, we don't have these old mechanisms.

The Piscean age was a time focused on hierarchy, authority, patriarchy, and external guidance, where people sought direction from leaders, institutions, and established systems. People were not encouraged to be autonomous and there was an out-of-balance masculine energy. In contrast, the Aquarian age brings us self-empowerment, unity, and direct connection to Source. Here we learn to take responsibility for our own spiritual growth and our role in the collective consciousness. It is about collaboration and heart-centred living, and we see the rise of the divine feminine that brings us into balance.

Choose one news story or issue to follow at a time. When we watch the news we are bombarded with a range of stories. If you want to help a particular situation as service work, follow that and stay in your light.

Here is a shorter visualization prayer you might like to use:

> *Dear Archangel Michael, please come to me now.*
> *I call upon your deep blue dragons to go straight to . . .*
> *(name place/person/people/situation).*
> *Please clear the lower energies there now so*
> *the light can shine again.*
> *Please assist each person involved in healing and learning*
> *from the situation for the highest good. I send the cosmic*
> *diamond flame to each person now and they are held*
> *within this and feel its warmth and light.*
> *Thank you. So be it.*

Our Devices and How They Affect Our Energy

If you have a smartphone, notice how it feels when it's in your hand. Do you have cords that tether you to it?

Here's a brief look at what's in the phone that might present cords:

- Conversations with any number of people. How many people do you message in a day typically? Are you in a lot of group chats? Do strangers or people you don't know very well send you random messages?

- News notifications. For a while, the news was crashing into my phone, until I realized how I'd accidentally allowed a certain website to send me notifications and how to stop it.

- Marketing—you are a potential customer to millions of businesses. Many are constantly being marketed to when using their phones.

- Unfinished business. Did you start to learn a language, or train your brain, for example, and then decided now's not the time, and you still have the app on your phone?

It can be helpful to clear your phone of apps you're not using, so that when you look at them they're not draining you or making you feel guilty or torn in some way. Tune in and see how you feel about each app. Similarly, if you have a notepad app on your phone, does it contain lots of old lists that aren't needed any more? Apply this same principle to all of your devices. Ask Archangel Michael's deep blue dragons to clear your devices and protect them.

Remedies for Being Overly Helpful

If you're the caring, helpful sort, watch out for over-volunteering, where you are run ragged trying to help others. This isn't balanced and will pull you off your path. It's a wonderful thing to be able to help others and your community, but not to become over-invested in other people's agendas and leave nothing for yourself. This is martyrdom and it moves you away from your highest blueprint. It is also being stuck in masculine energy. To balance the masculine and feminine energies, remember to receive. Stop and listen, to spirit, to your intuition. Accept help, gifts, and favours. Receive a compliment with grace. Know your limits.

Chioma wanted to reconnect with herself but found she had little time for anything. Not only did she have four school-age children, she helped care for her aging parents and volunteered in her community. She was a kind-hearted soul who loved to help others. But at times she felt resentful. She told me, "I feel like there is no *me* left. I am always there for others, but I get no time." She felt bad about saying these things, but she deeply wanted to connect with herself and feel more balanced.

She asked, "Angels, how can I make more time for myself?" and at first she didn't receive any thoughts or insights. But then a friend rang, asking her to come on a trip with her. It was so out of the blue, and at first she said no, she was too busy. Then she remembered her question to the angels, and rang her friend back to say she would like to come, but she needed to make some arrangements. Of course, the help she needed was easy to organize when she gave herself permission and made space.

Deceased Loved Ones

Angels, how do I connect with my deceased loved one?

Know and respect that they are travelling now. Become as light
and free as a bird in your spirit and connect with them through
your love in gratitude for them. Send them a ray of pure joy from
your heart.

Grief and Heartache

If you are feeling heartbroken over the death of a loved one, I want to
begin by sending you the biggest angel hug. Archangel Chamuel is wrapping loving wings around you now and comforting you. Receive it. The
angels want to help us to process grief and to feel that connection with
the loved one in a way that makes sense for us.

It's hard to imagine sometimes, but you came into this world alone,
even if you are one of twins. All the loved ones we are privileged to meet
in this lifetime are only passing through, even though we may have met
them in different lifetimes and may well meet them in another. We don't
own anybody and nobody can own us. Precious soul, you are so loved by
so many angels and loving guides you would scarcely believe it, and when
we leave our physical body we can finally see this again. Just as your loved
one can see it now.

A Conundrum

The conundrum of deep grief seems to me that we worry that if we do
not feel pain it might mean that we are somehow disloyal to the loved
one, so therefore we must carry the burden of pain and heartache relent-
lessly to prove our love. This can affect any relationship, but I see it very
acutely when a parent has lost a child.

Rhonda Byrne explains in *The Power* that to feel your deceased loved one you need to be on the frequency of love. We can't feel them on the frequency of fear and pain. Raise your vibration with gratitude for the loved one. Look for things you're grateful for right now, look for beautiful memories you may have of that person of their time on Earth. Grief can have people trapped in time, unable to be in the present for fear that it just isn't acceptable without that loved one here. Yet in truth our loved ones are as light as ever. I like to think they would wish for us to make the best of our time here on Earth.

Set Them Free

We none of us know while we are in our earthly bodies what it's like on the other side. By setting someone free, you aren't saying you don't care about them any more, but you are no longer tethering them to you. If we are meant to incarnate for a certain length of time and when we die this is our time, then it makes sense that we, the surviving loved ones, should let the other go with love. Missing the loved one is natural, but notice if you are speaking to them or about them in your head as though you simply don't accept or forgive them being gone. These sorts of thoughts, when repeated over and over, are very painful and may tether the energy of a loved one to you in an unhealthy way.

Tapping Exercise to Cope with Repetitive Painful Thoughts

Using the tapping points overleaf, say the person's name and go around the points gently and slowly, taking comfortable breaths and being aware of the sensations in the body. You can expand if you like, to say, *I love you, I miss you, or I release you with love*, or any other phrases that make sense to you. But do this tapping whenever you can when these painful thoughts come about, to break the pattern and release the stuckness.

If doing this on your own isn't helping, reach out and get help. This goes for any repetitive thoughts connected to grieving that pull you down. Life is too precious to stay stuck.

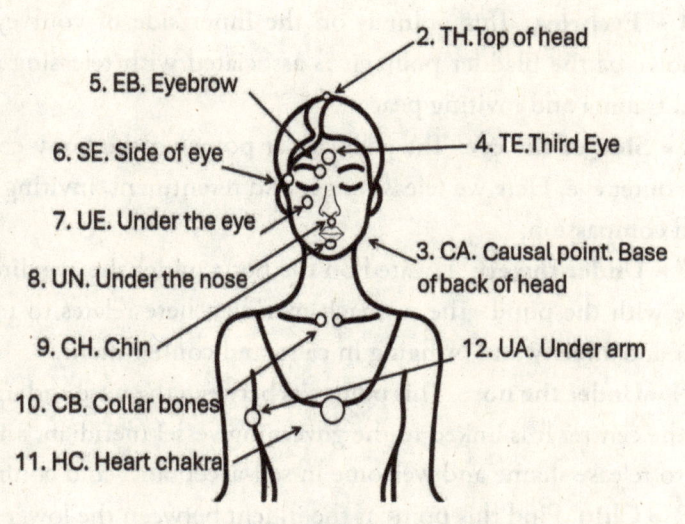

5. EB. Eyebrow

6. SE. Side of eye

7. UE. Under the eye

8. UN. Under the nose

9. CH. Chin

10. CB. Collar bones

11. HC. Heart chakra

2. TH.Top of head

4. TE.Third Eye

3. CA. Causal point. Base of back of head

12. UA. Under arm

Fig.4: The EFT Contact Points

This is the sequence of the tapping routine with point explanation:

1. **PA = Palms awake**. Have your hands laid on your lap with palms upward facing. Pause here, relax, and as you tune into the angels, invite them to connect with you.

2. **TH = Top of your head**. This is the crown chakra point, your connection to the higher chakras and the higher realms, including the angelic realms and unity consciousness.

3. **CA = Causal**. The causal point right near the occipital lobe. It coincides with the Alta major chakra that allows kundalini energy to flow and connects to the higher throat chakra as well. In Chinese medicine this point is also connected to balance, and calms the spirit and emotions and supports brain function. Cup the hand here, rather than tapping.

4. **TE = Third eye**. Located in the centre of the forehead. Supports clearing unhelpful aspects of the third eye—things we've been picturing in our mind that aren't good—and creating new pictures of what we want to manifest.

5. **EB = Eyebrow**. This point is on the inner side of your eyebrow. Known as the bladder point, it is associated with releasing sadness and trauma and inviting peace.
6. **SE = Side of the eye**. The gallbladder point on the bony corner of the outer eye. Here we release anger and resentment, inviting insight and compassion.
7. **UE = Under the eye**. Located on the bone under the eye directly in line with the pupil. The stomach meridian here relates to releasing fear and anxiety and bringing in calm and contentment.
8. **UN = Under the nose**. This point sits between the nose and upper lip in the centre. It is linked to the governing vessel meridian, and helps us to release shame and welcome in self-acceptance and confidence.
9. **CH = Chin**. Find this point at the indent between the lower lip and the fleshy part of the chin. It is the central vessel meridian which helps us to release confusion and grow self-confidence and clarity.
10. **CB = Collarbone**. Located around where the knot of a tie would sit. It is linked to the kidney point helping us to let go of anxiety and to feel more determined and also grounded.
11. **HC = Heart Chakra**. Place your hands, palms flat, lovingly over your heart centre. Focus on engaging the heart, allowing love to flow into this situation or request. You can say or think the words, "from my heart."
12. **UA = Under the arm**. Spleen point helps us to release worry and connects again to the heart chakra – imagine softening and flowing into love here. Allow a deep sigh.
13. **PA = Palms awake**. At the end of your tapping round or rounds, use palms awake again and listen to what guidance comes through. Guidance can come through now or later as thoughts and ideas that feel light and inspiring. Or it might just be a time to be still and let the work you have just done settle in.

Complicated Grief and Healing
the Conflicted Heart

It is said that the more complex or troubled your relationship with your deceased loved ones, the trickier grieving can be. This is because we are confused about how to feel. For example, if you are/were angry and resentful towards the person, as well as loving them deep down, it can seem as though there's unfinished business. People can carry guilt about those feelings. The thoughts can go around and around in a seemingly endless painful cycle. Each time they think of the person can feel like a stab to the heart, a confused bundle of being sorry they're gone and a concoction of other unpleasant feelings. In some cases you may feel just anger and resentment, because the relationship was so painful but the person was close to you.

You can talk to this person even though they're not here physically. It doesn't matter if you don't know if they can hear you or not. Tell them how you feel. I do recommend talking to someone if you are suffering from complex grief. I have worked with many clients on this topic and there is a lot we can do with energy work and even just getting those feelings off your chest. Just as I write this now, a rainbow is appearing and the light outside is becoming soft and ethereal. As though the angels and a thousand deceased loved ones want to get their message across.

Life on Earth can be very tough for all of us, no matter where you are born and into which family. Like boot camp. You came here because you wanted to do some big learning. You don't remember that now—most of us don't at least. But there's a queue to get here and we're lucky. When we arrived we quickly forgot our mission and journey to date. It is through meditation and talking to the angels that we start to remember. Your deceased loved one is much lighter since they've left their body. They don't carry the same burdens.

Trapped Spirits and Ghosts

If you feel that there are trapped spirits in your home, you can always help them by calling an expert—Archangel Michael.

Jeremiah told me his house felt haunted and he believed it was his aunt-in-law, who owned the house previously and was always hostile to him. He felt a heavy energy, especially in the hallway at the front door, and said things got moved around and broken. His five-year-old daughter couldn't sleep well and would frequently wake up crying and shouting. His relationship with his wife was strained and, in heated arguments, she kept mentioning divorce. He desperately wanted things to work out and for them to stay together, but he got an increasing feeling of doom. Sometimes at night he even felt a presence right next to him.

Then he chanced upon a friend one day who he knew from primary school. They got chatting and the friend told him he now worked with angels and energy healing. Jeremiah ended up telling him about the heavy feeling in the house, and the friend told him about how to work with Archangel Michael. At the time, Jeremiah felt sceptical, but it was a huge coincidence to meet this friend and that they would have such a conversation, so he didn't discount it.

Afterwards, he remembered his mother's faith in the angels and he began to call in Archangel Michael to protect him and his family and to remove any entities or spirits from the home. He contacted the friend and the man gave him a protective prayer. Jeremiah said this protective prayer once a day and lit a candle for his aunt-in-law, sending her good wishes. Even though he still harboured resentment, he opened his heart to her and wished her safe travels on the next part of her journey.

After just three days his wife suggested that they all go away on a holiday. It was so out of the blue he could scarcely believe it. She said she'd always wanted to go to Donegal on Ireland's west coast, so they went, and they got along better than they had done in years. She smiled and laughed a lot, and he saw the spark he used to see in her, and she in him.

When they returned, he smelled the scent of roses when they entered the house, even though there were no roses in the house. He had got

> *Dear Archangel Michael,*
> *Under the Law of Grace please help me now.*
> *Surround me and my family*
> *with your protective deep blue light.*
> *Fill my house with your love and wisdom.*
> *Escort any lingering spirits or entities over*
> *to the light now.*
> *I surrender my fear and replace it with*
> *love and gratitude.*
> *I am completely protected, surrounded,*
> *and infused with light.*
> *My family are completely protected,*
> *surrounded, and infused with light.*
> *Our home is completely protected,*
> *surrounded, and infused with light.*
> *Amen.*

used to almost bracing himself in the past whenever he entered the front door, like he was going into battle. But he noticed how relaxed his body felt this time, and how the light shone in rays through the patio doors. It was a beautiful sunny day and he opened all the windows. His wife commented, "It feels different in here." His daughter said she could see sparkles everywhere and began dancing around the house.

From this time the couple continued to get along better. They made some home improvements and bought more house plants, which are good at raising the energy. Jeremiah set an intention daily to keep light in the home, and began to learn how to meditate. Their daughter began to sleep through the night and was more relaxed. Jeremiah planted an apple tree and a rose bush in their garden, silently dedicating them to his deceased aunt-in-law, to honour her. And in the hallway he put a glass crystal that makes rainbows all over the walls when the sun hits it.

19

Lemurian Planetary Healing

The Lemurians once incarnated on Earth and were a lot like angels, rather than humans. They were of a very high vibration. They could teleport and never harmed the planet in what they did to survive and enjoy life. Before their era ended, they sent their powerful light into the planet, which then solidified into the Lemurian crystals, for us to work with now.

Lemurian Crystals

Lemurian crystals hold the healing energy of Lemuria and can be activated remotely as well as by those trained to use them for the benefit of the planet. If you are guided to buy your own Lemurian crystal, see it as a commitment to work with the Lemurians, but know that you don't need to have one physically to work with them. A Lemurian quartz wants to work with those who are connected to the Lemurians. That said, if you have Lemurian crystals and are not using them, it's possible they are being activated remotely anyway.

Mother Mary overlit the Lemurian era, and at this time she was known as Ma Ra. There is a seventh-dimensional chakra at the heart of Mother Earth called Hollow Earth and in here a Lemurian dimension from where you can access the dragon kingdom. The dragons have a deep love of Mother Earth with their big, open hearts and assist with Lemurian healing, as do the unicorns.

Lemurian Connections

If you have a deep love of nature and animals and you value living gently on the planet, you may well be connected to the Lemurians. I highly recommend training in Lemurian planetary healing with the Diana Cooper

School of White Light if you are interested in learning how to work with these crystals. You can also enjoy taking part in this healing through my workshop at **https://angeleft.com/resources** —this is designed for beginners as well as those who are experienced.

Once I was guided to gift a dolphin a Lemurian crystal, and so I did. I went out on the tour boat with a group and I dropped the Lemurian quartz into the sea at Dingle Bay, where the beautiful, generous dolphin, Fungie, used to swim. Even though he was wild, he visited humans in the same spot every day from 1983 to 2020. Fungie's beautiful message to humanity rang loud and clear: open your hearts. People of every age and from all over the world would come and see Fungie; they'd laugh and smile and feel the joy he brought. Perhaps he was a Lemurian dolphin. I like to think he worked with the Lemurian quartz, and that it is still there now doing its work and being activated when people activate the Lemurian crystals.

It is said that a community of Lemurians still live today in the subterranean city of Telos, underneath Mount Shasta, California, and some people who are connected to Lemuria visit them in meditation. Archangel Gabriel's etheric retreat is also above Mount Shasta.

Beloved Mother Earth, how can I help you?

Use your gifts and talents. Access your creative mind. Above all, raise your frequency and help others to do the same. In a high vibration, humans naturally want to love and respect me.

If you are passionate about helping the planet, take some time now to list things you are good at and enjoy doing. Positive change for our planet can come from speakers, writers, website designers, artists, creatives of all kinds, gardeners, swimmers, meditators, builders, designers, scientists, researchers . . . and all kinds of people from all walks of life, and from all over the world.

Positive Vision and Actions for the Planet

The angels told me, "Eco anxiety, just like any other anxiety or fear, is on the lower part of the scale. Keep coming back to the scale. Taking action is on the higher end, especially when you do so with love and with a vision for success."

It's perfectly understandable to be worried about the way humans have treated the Earth, and yet worrying doesn't help and sends you into a spin. In this space, it's very difficult to do something that makes a positive difference. Worrying or being angry navigates us toward blaming and separation consciousness. To blame those who do harm is also very understandable, and yet it generally makes people dig their heels in even more.

It's my understanding that we need to learn to work together. There are many gifts and talents in the pool of the almost eight billion people that we are. Your actions can inspire others and this, as well as being in a high vibration, may be our superpower when it comes to helping Mother Earth, who is an old soul with wisdom beyond our comprehension. She doesn't wish for you to be ashamed of your human self, but to reach for the higher consciousness choices and hold the vision of the new, golden age that is unfolding. Listen and she will whisper to you. She will guide you.

Nature has all the answers, so spending time in nature will also help. Pick one thing to start with and treat yourself with kindness. We need to raise our vibration, hold our vision, and take wise actions. By asking questions we can manifest change. Of our angels and of our fellow people, and decision-makers. When canvassers come to your door, ask about the planet. Email or ring them and ask. If lots of people are asking then they know this is high on the agenda. See page 204 for a Huna prayer to help the environment.

Visualization to Connect with Lemuria

1. Ask Archangel Michael to clear you and the space you are in completely of lower energies and to bring in high-frequency energy. Only high-frequency energy and beings are now permitted within this space.

2. Breathe in golden-white Lemurian light that is being poured over you like a waterfall of light coming from Source and the Lemurians now.

3. Mother Mary is placing her aquamarine protective cloak of light around you. See it expanding and sealing the outer edges of your aura.

4. A great host of unicorns are approaching you. They make a circle around you and direct their swirling horns of silver light towards you. Feel this beautiful blessing.

5. Feel your heartbeat connecting with the beating of the cosmic heart. Know that you are connected in love and the high-frequency grid to all that is.

6. A Lemurian dragon is approaching you. She lands in front of you and raises her head. Make contact with her. Look into her beautiful loving crystal eyes. Climb up onto her back. Feel her luminous crystal scales under your hands. Fly with her through the dimensions, all the way into the Lemurian part of Hollow Earth.

7. She brings you to a great room made of crystal; many shards of light fill the room and you see many dragons, unicorns, and very tall beings of light there. These are the Lemurians. One great being steps forward to welcome you. You are invited to light a candle and place it at the great altar. Set the intention to connect with the Lemurians for the highest good of Earth.

8. In the very centre of the room is a seat made of crystal, the seat of wisdom, and you are invited to sit on it. It is very comfortable and you feel a very beautiful energy enfolding you.

9. Many beings are gathering around you and showering you with love and healing. As they do, tune in to any guidance you are receiving in this magical space; it will help you on your journey with the Lemurians, should you choose to work with them in your life. Take some time here. They are showing you how life is in Lemuria, and the wisdom we can use now from this.

10. Your dragon invites you to come back now. You get up from the chair and thank the many loving beings. You climb onto your dragon's back and she brings you up and through the dimensions again. All the way back to where you started. You lower yourself back to the Earth and feel your feet firmly planted and connected to Earth and back in your protected space filled with glorious new knowing. Thank your dragon.

11. Write down any messages you'd like to remember. Drink some water.

PART FIVE

RELATIONSHIPS

Improving Your Relationships

Angels, how can I improve my relationships?

Love yourself and then you see the light in others. When out of
balance, working too hard, not enough self-care, you see others'
faults. Your relationships are a mirror. Kindness, gentleness,
compassion, and love are what heal and transform.

The things we see in others are also things we recognize in ourselves. Our
shadow side, those parts of us we find difficult to love, are sometimes
harder to see.

Be the one to love first. Many people have healed what were terrible
relationships by letting go of all ego and being the one to love first. This
means bypassing the resentment, the "story" of why the other person is
wrong and just loving them anyway, exactly as they are. We can do this
more easily the higher we are up the vibrational scale. If we are below 4
it can feel impossible. But above 7 it's easy. Bring your vibration higher if
you want to do this.

Loving someone else unconditionally means not getting mad again
when they don't respond well right away. It's being patient. If it doesn't
work today, try it again tomorrow. And if they ultimately don't reciprocate your kindness, respect their free will to choose that too.

For this chapter, we will look at family relationships, friendships, and
work relationships.

Improving All Relationships

Do you find that all relationships in your life are equal, or are there some
people who raise you right up the scale and others who seem to pull you
down? How are you responding to the latter? Are you avoiding them,

speaking ill of them, expecting them to annoy or disappoint you? If you are, you are contributing to the relationship being bad and lowering your own frequency. When we speak ill of others, regardless of the situation, it pulls our frequency down. If you need to speak about something bad someone has done, because of a very serious situation that requires intervention for example, take the appropriate action and then do something afterwards that will help raise your vibration. And ask, *Angels, how have I attracted this and what is it showing me?*

Think for a moment of several of your relationships and how they are functioning just now. Can you find some that feel clear and uncomplicated? Sometimes our relationship with a more distant relative is a less complex one that feels clear and easy. Our immediate family relationships or our partners can be the most complicated as they have so many layers and the stakes are high. As can our relationship with colleagues or a manager, but in a different way.

Beautiful Challenge

The beautiful challenge in our relationships is to learn the lesson of detachment. Detach yourself from the drama and you have learned the lesson and it won't keep on repeating. Each time you become triggered by someone else's behaviour, be grateful for the learning and willing to look at it. This is how to evolve. Think of this person as an actor sent from heaven to test you until you learn the lesson. What are they teaching you? Patience? Assertiveness? Boundaries? Self-belief? Or simply how to remove yourself from the situation? There is always learning, so each time seek to be grateful and take responsibility.

Victim Talk

When you hear someone or yourself complaining about another, know that this is the victim archetype speaking. Notice the feeling in your body if and when you do. Those who have mastered the lesson don't need to talk about other people. Gossip doesn't interest them because they know it only lowers their frequency and it's most helpful to see even the most challenging people through the eyes of compassion, or simply move your focus towards something else.

If you are in a conversation with someone else who is doing this and trying to get you to agree and conspire with them, find ways to change the subject. Look them in the eye, smile, and ask, "How are you doing?" Try asking them questions about themselves, or reflect back to them a wonderful quality they have.

Visualization to Soften a Complex Relationship with the Ascension Flame of Love and Harmony

Lady Venus governs the Ascension Flame of Love and Harmony, which is bright pink and carries codes of pure love. When you call this in, you are connected with the Cosmic Heart and you experience serenity and beautiful relationships.

Think of someone with whom your relationship is strained or complex, that you would like some help with for this exercise. You can also call to mind a famous person whom you have never met if you feel you have cords of resentment to them and would like to soften those.

1. Relax your body and invite in Lady Venus, Goddess of Love. Breathe in bright pink light. See this filling up your cells and your energy fields.

2. Lady Venus touches your heart. Breathe and feel your heart respond and expand.

3. Now feel this ascension flame flowing right down through your stellar gateway chakra, the soul star, the causal, the crown, the third eye, the throat, the heart, the solar plexus, the navel, the sacral, the root, and the earth star chakra. See them all expanding out with pink light. Bathe in love for yourself.

4. Now send the pink Ascension Flame of Love and Harmony to this other person from your heart to theirs. See them receiving it and it starting to fill up their whole body, radiating out from the heart. See them relaxing and feeling the light as it works through all of their energy fields and chakras.

5. Focus on the heart connection between you. The flame is cleansing and breaking up old patterns, limiting beliefs, fears, old hurts, and resentments so that both of you are free from these lower-energy limitations.

6. Now see the relationship as clear and bright. How do you act and feel differently?

But What About Narcissists?

I have much compassion for people who feel so aggrieved by another that they believe them to be narcissists. Yet, it's important to note that narcissism is a label that encourages victim dialogue. Any notion making the other person fundamentally wrong and you right is veering into the territory of not learning the lesson. It may feel satisfying at the time to surmise that this person who has done you all of this wrong is flawed and has something amiss with them, but this doesn't help raise your frequency. Things can't evolve for you until you master whatever it is the universe is trying to teach you.

If this is going on in your life, I challenge you to instead think of the flawed behaviour of the other person as their lowest-vibrational behaviour, and refrain from using labels for the person themselves. In these human bodies, we are all capable of bad, unhelpful, silly, selfish, cruel, spiteful (etc.) behaviour on the lower end of the scale. And we have no need or desire for those behaviours when we're at the higher end of the scale. By naming, thinking about, talking about, and ruminating on the bad behaviour of others we only pull ourselves into a sticky vortex of lower frequency. Judgement pulls us this way.

So the focus is to raise our frequency and keep visualizing what we want—not vengeance, or the other person getting their comeuppance, but us feeling the way we really want to feel. This may be exceptionally challenging if the person is someone you have to deal with a lot and can't seem to get away from. But keep coming back to *you*. What do you love? What makes your heart sing? If you raise your vibration high enough, this person simply can't bother you any more, because you will no longer be a match and therefore you will repel their bad behaviour, even if you are somehow tied to them through, for example, being related or being parents of the same child. Anything they do that is less than love goes under your high-vibrational radar—that is, it doesn't bother you because you are anchored in love and delight. Make this your mission and get help if you need it.

Keep asking questions . . . *Angels, how can I help myself to rise above this situation? How can I attract the help I need?*

Fire Dragon Healing to Release Unhelpful Labels and Victimhood

1. In a safe, private place, on a piece of paper that nobody else will find, write down all the unhelpful things you have been saying or thinking about the other person. Feel free just this once to use all of those names, phrases, and such. Really let rip.

2. Now invoke the fire dragons to burn up these old phrases and names. Physically burn it, or if this is not possible tear or cut it up into many, many tiny pieces and then bury it, asking the earth dragons to transmute it into compost and love now.

3. Now take another piece of paper and write about how you would like to feel and be. You can release or keep this one. Release it if it means you will feel absolutely free to write anything you want.

Examples:

I am confident.

I am steady.

I am wise.

I feel brave.

I feel grounded.

I am so grateful that I feel so happy.

My life is blissful and fun.

I laugh a lot every day.

I feel full of vitality and bliss.

I stand firm in my own high vibration and have compassion for others knowing that everyone is doing their best.

I attract amazing opportunities.

I know what to do.

I feel wise and accomplished.

4. If you like to draw or paint, create an image that represents your happiness and joy. Repeat as necessary. Where you put your focus is where things will grow.

Earth Angel Parents

I am using the word parent here, but I mean both parents and guardians. This chapter may also help teachers and assistants, others who work with children, and other relatives who have a relationship with a child or children and who care for them.

Angels, how can I do the best for my child?

When you connect with the higher aspect of your child, what do you know about them? This soul who chose to incarnate with you. You can speak to their higher selves or guardian angels any time you wish for guidance. See yourself as a vibrant, healthy parent who provides a safe, calm energy space to be around where your child can thrive.

When we are calm, or in flow, we demonstrate this to our child. Do you find yourself worrying about your child? If you do, seek to break the habit. There is a myth I often hear, especially of mothers, that it is a mother's job to worry. This is an old third-dimensional belief and unhelpful. While it may be nature's way for a mother to feel anxious trying to protect her child, it's rather our job to come back to centre and demonstrate how to be in flow. What you model, your child can follow. Whether they do or not depends on many variables, but doing your best is the best you can do.

Transitioning from Helicopter Parent to Earth Angel Parent

Helicopter parenting is another type of anxious parenting. Not trusting your child to make decisions or to try things out for themselves and over-supervising them. If you catch yourself doing this, be compassionate. This was perhaps modelled for you by one of your parents. Or perhaps the contrary; you felt as though there weren't boundaries or safety and so you've been seeking to create very strong supervision for your child so the same cannot happen to them. Think of making the transition from helicopter parent to earth angel.

The earth angel parent is protective and also trusting, seeing the beautiful, radiant higher self of the child and their exquisite light as they explore their surroundings and learn how things work and how to be safe. Earth angel parent knows when to delegate, e.g. "Archangel Michael, please protect my child at school today. Please flow your light into his throat chakra so that he can stand up to others. Please Archangel Jophiel, help to clear her mind so she can study."

It might help you to write out the main worries you have about your child if you worry about them a lot. You can destroy this afterwards. But get it down on paper. Then, see if you can make an affirmation for the positive opposite. You can say or even talk and tap on these positive opposites, using Angel EFT.

Examples

- My child cannot cope with peer pressure . . .
  I trust that my child is becoming assertive and strong.

- My ex-partner is a bad influence on my child . . .
  My child chose the perfect parents for their soul growth and I trust that all is well and in divine order. I invite support for my child now.

- My child isn't studying for exams and won't do well in life . . .
  I trust that my child will learn all they need to know and live a wonderful and fulfilling life.

- I am so worried about my child's special needs and not living a happy life . . .
  My child has chosen the perfect incarnation and is doing brilliantly on their journey.

Prayer to Protect Your Children

*In the name of God and All that is Light,
Under the law of Grace, I pray that my child is held
in the Christ Light today.*

*Archangel Michael please surround them in your protective
deep blue cloak and help them to learn to detach themselves
from any toxic situations and energies.*

*Archangel Metatron please surround them with your light. I
ask that Metatron's cube be brought right down through their
12 chakras to cleanse and clear their energy fields now to
help them to be their bright, radiant selves.*

*Archangel Zadkiel and Archangel Gabriel and Jesus, please
clear away any psychic clutter for my child with your
beautiful gold, silver, and violet flame. Let them radiate the
light out wherever they go in a way that feels good to them.*

*Archangel Jophiel please also clear me of worry and any
negative thoughts and help me to visualize the best for them.*

And so it is. Amen.

Prayers, such as the above, can be very helpful. If you like, as an addition you can chant or use a mantra after saying this prayer to help you to maintain a high frequency and dissolve lower energies and thoughts from yourself.

I like *Om Gam Ganapataye Namaha*. This mantra is connected to the elephant god, Lord Ganesha—the remover of obstacles. As a parent, see him removing worry and clutter so that you can easily visualize your child safe, happy, and being their bright, amazing selves. We may carry over psychic debris from previous generations and family karma or ancestral patterns, so with intention this mantra can also help to clear this away.

Parenting in Flow

I remember when I had small children, going places could be stressful, trying to organize all the many things I needed to bring for a baby or toddler. Foods, drinks, playthings, changes of clothes, the list went on. My happiest memories of these times were when I was taking good care of myself. This way I was a happier, calmer parent and able to be in flow.

Do you take good care of yourself? What does it mean to you to do this? A nice measure of this is to make a wheel, like the wheel of life (see page 40), and list the segments of good self-care, so that you can measure them and see if anything could do with improving. Then you can make plans on how to start to better things.

Remember the question, how do I move up one place? Rather than how do I get to 10? If the number is low, this can feel overwhelming. If you worry that self-care means expense and time you don't feel is currently available, try doing some tapping, which is free and can be combined perfectly with minding a child. In fact, showing children how to tap is a gift to them also.

The Power of Words

As a writer and avid reader, I love words. Doing the work I do, I also acknowledge the enormous power that words have. When we ask open-ended questions, for example, we invite the other person to expand their answer. A closed-ended question that requires a simple yes or no is more restrictive, which is appropriate sometimes and not at others. Our words can be positive and welcoming of possibility and opportunity, or opinionated and diminishing, boxing us into lower-vibrational spaces. This is the same in our parenting, the way we speak to our children, about our children, about the world, and about ourselves. If we use words and expressions that are open to opportunity and positive, we model this for our children too.

If you find you speak quite negatively, have compassion for yourself. It was likely modelled for you by someone else. And either way, you have the choice to learn new ways. Our personalities are said to be a mix of nature and nurture, but I like to think we have the power to change pretty much any aspect of our personalities if we really want to. So if people around you say you are a worrier, you don't need to remain one.

Encourage children to work with powerful questions, whether to angels or of themselves.

- How could you help yourself feel better about this?
- What other ideas might work?
- How could we reach an agreement on this?
- What do you think might help this situation that you could do?

An Important Note

When we have children, at various points it brings up issues from our own childhood. This is because being a parent reminds us of our own childhood and what was modelled for us. If you have some trauma or difficult memories from your childhood, reach out and get help for it. You don't have to work on this alone, and support might be what is best for you.

The New Children

Many light beings are coming to Earth just now and the last couple of decades have seen an enormous number of very high-frequency souls being incarnated to help out. Please remember that, just like us, many children have forgotten what they're doing here and might be rebelling, as they are wondering, "What is this place?" The indigos, crystal, and rainbow children are but a few of what the New Age community are recognizing as these special souls.

Some will be placid, caring, and unusually mature. Others will wreak havoc as they find their bearings and rebel against the old structures that they find absurd. That tumultuous phase will pass; as a parent, see the brightest and best in them wherever you can. Make sure the boundaries are good and strong, yet enlightened, as some of them feel very unsafe in this phase. Teach them spiritual tools if they're open to them—and if they're not, know that they might be at a later time in their lives.

Many highly advanced spiritual children are being diagnosed as neurodivergent—as having autism, ADHD, dyslexia, etc. But the medical model's disparagement towards neurodivergence is now beginning to dissolve, and people are recognizing the wonder and brilliance of brains that work differently.

Wanted for Big Hollywood Blockbuster

1. Imagine you are an actor going for a big Hollywood part. You are acting the part of a calm, confident "earth angel" parent and the director hasn't provided a script—she's told you to create your own and the best one, acted the best, will get the role.

2. Take some time to design your own script. How do you speak and what do you say? You can choose whether to use your own and your child's name or make up names. What is the situation you are writing the script about? Perhaps you'd like to choose something that happened recently where you didn't feel like a confident parent, but this time you will act the part of a confident parent.

3. It might be helpful to imagine someone you admire for their confidence, imagining how they might have behaved in that situation, what they might say. Take your time with this exercise. And rehearse for the audition just like a real actor does. The more you practise being the calm, confident parent the more easily you will be able to "act" this way in real life, and soon with practice it will come to you more naturally.

I love this exercise and have recommended it in many situations, not just for parents. I have even used it to help myself to get into the sea for a dip on a cold day, acting the calm, brave Hollywood actor who doesn't flinch at all.

22

Family Harmony

Angels, how can I feel centred and confident when I'm around my family (of origin)?

Remember who you are. Your precious imprint that is unique to you no matter where you are or whomever you are with, is your soul essence.

When you come to your family of origin, do you feel like a child? Or do old family patterns, hierarchies, hurts, and wounds make themselves felt? You have the power to transcend the old ways now. With intention, you can carry yourself in the way of a steady and confident being. With presence, you can rise above any dramas that don't belong in your field any more. You are powerful.

The family of origin often reminds you of the challenges you experienced as a child. If you have siblings, you become as children. Sometimes the order of birth is a hierarchy in the family and, even though you might be long past being a child, you can feel as though you have fallen back into the role of being the youngest/oldest/middle and so on. But we are part of the organic whole, and if we change then the others have no choice but to change as well. Even if their change doesn't look like yours. At the very least they don't have that expectation of you any more if you refuse to go into the assumed role.

How would you like to be now, today, in your family of origin? If you have family members who trigger you, try to remember that at one point in the ethers you chose these people. And they are meant to teach you, even if their teaching challenges.

Exercise – Family of Origin and Who I Am Now

Write down: "Today (date) when I am with my family of origin I am so happy that I am . . ." Then see what flows. Avoid words like no longer, avoid, stop, even though, etc., as these are negations and harder for you to stop thinking about the things you no longer want to do/say/feel/experience.

Example:

"Today, the 4th of June, when I am with my family of origin I remember who I am. I love that I am confident and bright. I see the good in everyone. I am centred and grounded and I feel delighted with my life."

If there is someone in your family whom you would like to be able to forgive but it's been difficult, you can write to Archangel Chamuel and place this letter either under a crystal or somewhere sacred. Or bury it or burn it, and consider it released.

Archangel Chamuel helps you to heal the heart, and unforgiveness lodges in the heart, causing a block. It is worth exploring this if you want to experience radiant health. If the issue is very deep-rooted and complex, ask the angels to guide you to the right source of help.

Blended Families, In-Laws, and Others

Other family that we gather as life goes on but didn't start out with can also present important lessons for us. And it's great to be in your own energy and to rise to the challenge where it presents itself. There are plenty of jokes about in-laws and even the word seems to carry a wry smile and a presumption of difficulty, and yet it brings us back to basics again. Our simple tribal selves enjoy what is familiar, even if it's not ideal, as opposed to other tribes who do things differently.

If there's a person you struggle to connect with or accept, see yourself opening your heart to them. A little bit at a time if that's easier. If you are afraid they will hurt you or let you down, look also at your expectations of them. Learn to take responsibility for your thoughts. If you expect someone to insult you, disrespect you, or hurt you in some way, immediately you are sending an unconscious invitation to them to do exactly that.

Just like if you walk along, terrified you will slip, you are more likely to slip than if you walk along with care and confidence. Like a gymnast who goes to perform some fabulously difficult sequence, they create a picture of themselves doing this in their mind to execute the moves. Expect to be treated well and this is what you are welcoming.

Eleanor felt triggered by her sister-in-law for many years. She had a sense of being judged by her, and she often endured mean comments. Eleanor braced herself when they met, just waiting for her to say something barbed. When she started to read about angels and change her life, instead of sitting with resentment Eleanor wondered if she could transcend this relationship. Her self-esteem improved when she began her transformational journey with the angels. She began to heal many self-doubts and forgive herself for choices she'd made in the past that used to haunt her. One of her favourite angel tools was to imagine Archangel Gabriel placing her in a cocoon of white light. When she asked Archangel Gabriel how to manage any disrespectful comments from this woman, the reply that dropped into her mind was simply, "Ask her a question."

Eleanor no longer braced herself when she met her sister-in-law. And her sister-in-law respected her more and was less likely to make unwelcome remarks. If she did, instead of shrinking down into a ball of resentment and hurt, Eleanor questioned her about it, calmly and respectfully: "What do you mean when you say that?" The response was always courteous, and their relationship changed for the good.

If someone offends you, are you telling the story about it in your head over and over? It's good to protect yourself energetically, yet also look out for the learning. Ask the angels about the correct course of action and again and again, assist yourself in reaching for the highest thoughts.

Angels, how best might I deal with this situation?
Angels, how can I help to raise the frequency of my
relationship with . . . ?
Angels, how can I protect myself when I am around . . . ?
Angels, how can I learn to forgive . . . ?

Body Language

How are you carrying yourself when you are around people? Are you standing tall and straight? Or do you slouch, and turn slightly to the side as though protecting yourself? Is your head straight and upright or are you avoiding eye contact or glancing at the floor? Is your throat chakra open or constricted? We tend to trust people more when they have open, non-challenging body language. Experiment with this in the mirror. How your stance looks, and how you might like it to look instead if there's room to improve.

Expect the Best to Attract the Best

Using affirmations such as *all of my relationships are in perfect harmony* can help you to manifest this. There are suggestions for tapping rounds you can use to work on your relationships in my book *Angel EFT, Tap into the Angelic Realms with Modern Energy EFT*, as well as on my YouTube channel.

You may see a pattern in your relationships. It's rare for there to be just one person and nobody else that you struggle with. If a theme keeps coming up, e.g., I feel disrespected; I get insulted; I feel as though they don't like me; I am not accepted—these themes often pop up across our relationships but the volume is turned up louder in some relationships than others.

Be curious, and compassionate towards yourself. We are all only learning—and keep learning. We keep learning as long as we are on this planet. That is why we came here to this exquisite school called Earth.

Come Back to Frequency

Over and over again, ask the question, *how can I raise my frequency one place higher?* Come back to yourself. Observe your reactions to others with kindness, curiosity, and even a little humour sometimes. See the lighter side of life. If the other person were an animal, what animal would they be? If you were an animal, which animal would you be? Check in with yourself on the vibrational scale before, during, and after meeting people who challenge you. With intention, you will master being in a high vibration around them. And when you are, you are immune to other people's poor behaviour, because it's no longer a match for you, and under spiritual law it must cease or transmute into something else that is of a vibrational match.

Ask the question: *Angels, what is this person teaching me?* You can also ask for protection: *Archangel Zadkiel, please surround me in your protective violet light. I am totally loved and held in light. And so it is.*

Visualization with the Gold, Silver, and Violet Flame for Family

1. Ask St Germain and Archangel Zadkiel to come to you now and invoke the Violet Flame of Transmutation.

2. Ask Master Jesus to bring the Gold Flame of Wisdom and to invoke the Silver Flame of Grace and Harmony.

3. Invite the Gold and Silver Violet Flame to flow through you and from you to each member of your family, and then back along the generations.

4. See it flow like a large, shimmering thread of fiery light, easily and powerfully touching each person and giving them healing.

5. Now lovingly release all of them and ask the Gold and Silver Violet Flame to form a protective cocoon around the edge of your aura.

We don't know all the stories that have passed down the generations energetically. We are complex beings, and don't know even all of our own stories. But with this intention, you can help bring healing and break through blockages that have been passed down the generations because they had nowhere else to go and weren't resolved.

I have seen ancestors sighing with relief during this work, their body posture changing and such. Our family and ancestors are a powerful influence but they are not the only ones. We are free as individuals also.

Attracting a Loving Partner

Angels, how do I attract a wonderful partner?

Find yourself in your perfect alignment and imagine a loving partner is there with you. What qualities do you adore in your partner? What is their energy like? What activities do you enjoy together?

Take some time to write down all the things you love about this partner that you want to attract into your life.

If you already have your heart set on someone who doesn't reciprocate your feelings, know that the angels will never "make" someone fall in love with you. This would be taking their free will away from them.

Ask yourself instead what it is you adore about that person and ask for someone to come into your life with these wonderful qualities. If you have difficulty stopping obsessing about this one person, ask the angels, "Angels, what can I do to release this person with love?" Listen to the answer. You will have formed an unhealthy cord through your thinking and the angels can help you to cut and dissolve this. When you release someone you've been corded to in this way, it makes a space for the right person to come to you.

Go back to the scale and measure where you are when you think of attracting your wonderful partner. If you are high up on the scale it is no trouble for you to attract them. The higher you are, the easier it is.

Listen also to your internal dialogue about this. What are your beliefs about love, romance, and ideal partners? It's important to listen to these thoughts so that, if any are not supporting you, you can work on changing the narrative. Even what you playfully say among friends doesn't go unheard.

Gabi wanted to be in a relationship. She'd been single for over four years and, though she'd been enjoying single life, she now found herself desiring a partner. Her friends saw her as super strong, capable, and inspirational and she was embarrassed to tell them about her change of heart. So she denied that she was seeking a partner when she was with them and secretly joined dating apps. She felt confident and ready in herself, but when she spoke to her friends she played along with their chatter about being so lucky to be single and how a partner would only lead to so many compromises and unhappiness. Gabi did a lot of work on her vibration but still, nobody she met was anything like a good match.

She asked her angels, "Angels, what must I do to attract a wonderful partner," and the reply was, *watch your words*. She laughed at first, because she had written letters to the guardian angel of her future partner, done visualizations to heal and ready her heart, and changed the narrative in her head about being with someone. Then she realized she was still playing the same record when she was with her friends. She quickly told them about her plans. At first, they found this most amusing and teased her about it, but then they were very supportive.

The following week, a new member joined the community volunteering she was involved with, and they instantly got along and were soon in a wonderful relationship together. Gabi still liked living on her own, so they lived in separate homes, and it worked very well.

Limiting Beliefs and Thoughts about Attracting a Partner

The difference between a thought and a belief is that the belief is deeper, has anchored into your consciousness as a "truth," and you see the world through the lens of this belief. Notice, when you have thoughts about attracting a partner, how powerful they feel. But a thought that is not a belief will not carry much weight and is easy to dispel. Beliefs also have different depths, and the deeper-rooted ones take a little longer to reshape. But reshape you can, using your powerful intention and drawing in the loving support of the angels.

Here are some examples of limiting beliefs:

- It's hard for me to attract someone nice.
- My past relationship hurts are holding me back.
- My parents' dysfunctional relationship is what was modelled for me and that's affecting my experiences.
- I always attract the wrong type.
- Nobody will stay with me.
- I'll end up sabotaging my relationship.

If you identified any of your own or any of the above, now turn it around and write the positive opposite, for example:

- It's easy for me to attract someone nice.
- My past relationships have shaped and prepared me for the perfect relationship now.
- My parents' relationship has shown me what I *do* want in a relationship.
- I attract wonderful people easily.
- My partner will love being with and staying with me.
- I love learning ways to nourish and nurture my relationship.

If you do this work and take time over it, listen out over the next week to see if more insights occur. Keep making those positive opposite affirmations where needed. As an added extra, use Angel EFT while saying the affirmations, and imagine each time you do it acts as a spring-clean, clearing out the old, unhelpful beliefs and lining you up to the perfect vibration to attract your partner.

Fall In Love with Yourself

Are you loveable? If you cannot answer yes to this question, work on your relationship with yourself. If you have some healing to do, make this a priority. When you love yourself you naturally consider yourself loveable. Other people pick up on this and you become magnetic and attractive to your ideal partner. People can feel it if you have very low self-esteem and feel unloveable.

Sometimes you may see people who seem to worship themselves and be full of ego. This is not the same as self-love. This is a false front and a mask for insecurity. You can tell the difference because those people seem to want to steal the limelight, and have all eyes upon them. They are pulling energy from all around them, which does not come from a place of self-love. Quite the opposite.

Those who truly love themselves want the same for others and share their light and kindness freely. Self-love is being at ease with yourself and knowing how to take care of yourself. And when you love yourself then you can love others.

Angels, how do I love myself more?

Remember all the things you like about yourself. If you are finding fault with yourself a lot, come back to what you like. Sit with yourself. You were not meant to be perfect, to be free of flaws and mistakes. You came here to learn and you have a lot of light to give. Remember your light. Remember who you are. The Monad reminds you that you are part of a sacred team and that you are not alone. They urge you to open up to your light and your brilliance. Source is shining on you.

Self-love can be a lifelong journey. If you are tough on yourself, you can recover from this. Treat yourself as you would a beloved. You are precious and have a place on this planet. When you bring your vibration into its higher states you will see the best in yourself. In the lower states, everything seems wrong, not good enough and so on. You are good enough.

Can you say it? I am good enough. Say it regularly. I am good enough. You can say more positive affirmations, of course, but if your self-talk has been harsh begin with that.

Kindness towards yourself can occur in many ways. Maybe it is to treat yourself to something nice. Perhaps it's to soak your feet in warm, salt water with essential oils. Or declutter your living space so the energy improves hugely. Or maybe it's to say no to something that is taking up your time and not benefiting you. To decorate your bedroom and make your sleep space more lovely. To walk outside in bare feet. To practise *pranayama*. Perhaps it's to have a clear finish time for work if you are self-employed. You will know, so ask the question and see what comes up.

Angel Exercise – I am good enough

1. Take a deep breath and allow golden angelic light to flow into your being as you inhale. On each in-breath, it infuses every cell of the body, every part of your being.

2. Feel your guardian angel wrapping their wings around you, cocooning you now in brilliant white light. White light has every colour of the rainbow in it. Feel the softness of your guardian angel and tell them, "I am good enough." Sense their seeing you with love.

3. If emotions surface, breathe them through the body. Your guardian angel has placed you in a bubble of brilliant white light with the intention of self-love growing and expanding. They are whispering to you how wonderful you are. Your guardian angel can see your highest blueprint and potential. They see you with eyes of pure, unconditional love.

Say I am good enough to yourself every day, at regular intervals. Get support where you need it. If you are very hurt you may need extra help from someone who can support you to love yourself more.

As humans, we are complex beings and we can present in all sorts of ways as our vibration goes up and down. It's best not to make assumptions about others. To do so is known as mindreading, which none of us can truly do, and comes from a place of fear. Note, it is different to telepathy, which is something we will all soon begin to develop and strengthen as humanity evolves, and comes from a place of love. When we love ourselves we do not need to judge others. If someone triggers you, they are showing you something valuable about you that you can work with. The angels love to help us with these insights and our healing.

Healing the Back of the Heart Chakra
with Archangel Chamuel

1. To receive, we need an open heart chakra. Often we visualize the front of this chakra but might forget about the back. The front is where the heart shines out and sends love. The back is about receiving, including love from other people.

2. Close your eyes and call in Archangel Chamuel. Feel this archangel stepping into your aura, and notice their delicate pink light.

3. Ask for them to place angelic hands of light on both the front and the back of the heart chakra and to scan how the heart is energetically.

4. Ask Archangel Chamuel to remove any blocks front, back, or anywhere in the heart chakra now, and be aware of what happens. You may receive insights.

5. Relax and allow this healing to be done.

6. Stretch your arms out to the sides, bring them forward palms together outstretched in front of you, and curl the upper back slightly. Now bring the arms out to the sides again and even behind you a little if this is comfortable. Enjoy the stretch and feel your heart chakra physically opening. See the light shining in through it from the back, and your heart light shining out in all directions. If possible, gently roll your shoulders, forwards and then backwards.

7. Set the intention that your heart is ready for love and you easily attract your loving partner to you.

8. Thank Archangel Chamuel.

Make Space in Your Life for Your New Partner

What will you do differently when your partner is here? Rhonda Byrne suggests playing games with the law of attraction when attracting a partner, such as making space in your wardrobe for your future partner's clothes or sleeping on one side of the bed to make space for them. Setting the table for you both. Imagining that they are already in your life and feeling what's different in your home. Make space in your life for them. Feel the feeling of what it's like to share with a partner. Imagine what your plans might be. If you are not planning to share a home with a partner, think about how else you can prepare for them.

Visualize Spending a Day with Your Partner

Close your eyes and imagine you are with your wonderful new partner. You're out for the day, or maybe on a trip somewhere. You are in a beautiful location. Look around and see what's there. Feel the closeness and warmth between you. The joy. Open your heart fully and allow yourself to connect with this person. See your heart welcoming them in delight. Ask the angels to anchor all these joyful feelings in your being, so that they radiate out. This helps you to attract this partner. Say, *I am so grateful for my wonderful new partner*, and mean it.

24

Thriving Long-Term Loves

The angels delight in helping us if we are in a long-term relationship and want to improve it. We change over time, in all of our cells, our consciousness, personalities, and our being. We are growing each day and you might feel like a very different person from the one who met your partner if that was years ago. Some people stay in a relationship because it's easier to stay than it is to leave, but they are not happy. Yet sometimes even the most dreary or troubled relationship has the potential to be great. Your intimate relationship can be a gateway to your bliss. Create, create, create. Play games and see the change.

Archangel Chamuel, how do I rekindle the fire
in my relationship?

What thoughts do you have about your partner? Start to listen to your thoughts carefully. What am I saying about my partner and my relationship in my head? Have you developed habits of criticism? Or do you see faults more than you see your partner's attributes? Make a list of all the things you like and love about them. Train your thoughts towards this direction. Speak with kindness, the way you like to be spoken to.

Go back to Chapter 1, page 21, or refer to your vibrational scale. Where is your relationship on the scale just now? How might you help it to move to the next level on the scale today? It's hard to imagine if you are in a very negative spin, but you have a huge influence over your happiness.

Imagine for a moment that despite the confusion, lower thoughts and habits that have come in and perhaps been habitual for a long time now, your relationship has the potential to be 10 on the vibrational scale.

How might that look to you? How does it feel? If it's hard to imagine, try the next level up the scale and work your way up from there.

An important exception is if you are in an abusive or dangerous relationship that you understand at a soul level you should leave. In this case, ask the angels for their support in helping you to do so safely, and work on your vibration so that you are no longer a match and therefore will easily be propelled out of this situation. Reach out for help and be safe.

Start with Yourself

Because your thoughts and feelings are so powerful, you can make a huge improvement in your relationship in a very short space of time. The trick is only to realize this. Many people are waiting for the other person to change while complaining and thinking the worst. It simply doesn't work this way. If you have been having negative thoughts, practise writing out what the positive opposites might be.

- My partner and I have grown apart and have nothing in common anymore.
  There is so much I still haven't discovered in my partner and I'm excited about what each day brings.

- My partner annoys me so much.
  I love the way my partner . . . (insert something you appreciate or used to appreciate about them).

- My partner takes me for granted.
  I love finding ways to show my partner I am grateful for them.

Write down as many as you can of these. You don't need to write out the negative, just use it as a starting point to show you the positive opposite.

Has your partner ever given you a gift that you loved? Remember it now and the way you felt. Expand your heart and really focus on that nice memory. If you still have whatever it was, use it as an anchor, a portal to happy times that shows you how to create that happiness now. Use any photographs you have of times you were happy together. Put them somewhere you will see them.

Kind Words

Using kind words to your partner is a sure way to begin the process of improvement if you don't already do this. With our words also comes our body language, our tone of voice, our expression, and our energy imprint. Focus on bringing them all into alignment. Even if your partner retorts or is critical, try to let it flow over you. Maybe you've been in an unhealthy pattern with your communication with them and they've still got their armour on.

Stay focused on the goal. Notice the traps you may have been falling into in your thoughts, words, and actions. The games or the dance you've been in with your partner. See yourself as now rewriting the script and doing things differently. You are the leader of this new dance.

When you aren't with your partner, you can also imagine your kind, grateful words and intentions flowing straight to them, perhaps being delivered by angels. See them receiving this nice energy and looking around, wondering. Perhaps they realize it is from you.

Joy spoke to the angels each day and many aspects of her life were wonderful. Except for this one glaring thing: her relationship with her husband. She shrugged it off and said it didn't matter. There was no fixing her marriage but to separate was not practical. When a friend suggested she ask the angels to help her in her relationship, she didn't want to know at first. They had got into the habit of sniping at one another. Old wounds were regularly opened up with the comments they made, which acted like arrows.

One day Joy was with a friend and their partner, and she noticed how kind they were to one another. She felt a stab of sorrow in her heart, and she wondered what that would be like for her. She asked, "Angels, is there any way of bringing my relationship with my husband one place up the scale?" Joy honestly expected radio silence. But the immediate thought came to her of the card she'd picked that morning, from Diana Cooper's card set, *The Magic of Unicorns*. It was about the ascension flames, and one of them was the Ascension Flame of Love. So she read the message again and asked, "Dearest Quan Yin, Archangel Chamuel, and the Light Beings of Andromeda, please come to me now and enfold me in the Ascension Flame of Love. Guide me in my marriage to have a more loving outlook. Go to my husband as well, if his soul permits it." Tears pricked her eyes, and she felt an unexpected wave of tenderness. Things began to improve. Her words were kinder and she was more patient with him. Her husband began to follow suit, and their love began to flourish once more. Joy kept saying the prayer each day for a month and, by the end of this time, they were closer than they had been in many years and enjoyed spending time together.

Tender Gesture and Touch

A small gesture, such as placing your hand briefly on your partner's shoulder or back, for example, can communicate a lot. How are you just now in this regard? Do you touch your partner or does the very thought of it make you recoil? Notice how you are and reflect on this and how you would like things to be. I believe we each have healing in our hands. Those who have trained in energy healing will know this from their training and have received attunements. But it's possible that everybody naturally has healing in their hands, whether or not they are aware of it.

Send a Ball of Light to Your Partner's Heart

1. Place your hands opposite one another in front of you and draw them closer together, slowly, then slowly apart. Can you feel the energy?

2. Ask the angels to pour light, a colour you like perhaps or golden angelic light, into a ball between your hands. You are creating, with the angels, a healing sphere of light.

3. Take a few minutes to feel it getting stronger and brighter. See the angels pouring lots of blessings into it.

4. Now pour love into it from your heart.

5. Think of one thing you are grateful for about your partner and add this to the ball also.

6. Send the ball of light to your partner's heart. See them receiving it.

Repeat as many times as you wish.

Persistence

While you can change things very quickly by doing this work, you also need to keep it up. Let it be your new habit. Commit to 21 days. Over time, you'll notice the old way doesn't fit any more.

Make Yourself a Channel for Love

1. Place your hands on your heart centre and breathe in deeply.

2. Feel the energy of your hands on your heart. Does your heart feel open or closed, or part open? Does your heart swell with love or does it feel achy with disappointment and grief?

3. Ask Archangel Chamuel to fill your heart with soft rose light.

4. Quan Yin is joining you as well and she is clearing your heart centre with her powerful energy. Helping you to release any hurt, disappointment, or heaviness in the heart centre.

5. You are becoming a channel for love.

6. See how your energy changes. You may be aware of colours surrounding you and shining out from the heart.

7. Now make a heart connection with your partner, and send them unconditional love. See it going like a ray of light from your heart to theirs.

8. Do this each day. Affirm: I am open to love.

PART SIX

YOUR SUPERPOWERS

Decluttering to Make Way for Amazing

When we have physical clutter, mess, and untidiness it serves as a big drain on our energy. It affects our abundance and potentially blocks the healthy flow of many aspects of life. If you follow the principles of Feng Shui you will know that the areas of your home represent areas of your life, a lot like the chakras.

How does the space you are in feel? Wherever you are, just notice how it affects your energy. Are you indoors or outdoors? Are there things around you, or open spaces? How is that for you? Is there something you can do right now to improve the space you're in if it's not feeling the best? Now think of your home. The room you sleep in. The place you prepare and eat food. The bathroom. The living space. Is it sparkling and uplifting or do things weigh on you?

Clutter and mess in the home is a base chakra issue. In the base chakra is also our relationship with money. I have literally found envelopes of money when decluttering, but also money has flowed better in many ways when I have done this. Many spiritual people find the base chakra the most challenging to keep in balance. Perhaps it doesn't seem as interesting as the exciting third-eye chakra, or the glowing causal. And yet when it's neglected we can't live our best life. Propel yourself into action using a timer—give yourself a set amount of time to focus solely on this. If 25 minutes is too much, try 11, or 5. In my opinion, the number of minutes doesn't really matter, it's the consistency of showing up that counts.

Angels, how do I learn to declutter and be tidy?

Make it a project to add this quality to your being. Have fun finding ways, play games. See it not just as physical matter but as mental chatter also, and old memories that are not uplifting. Distractions and old news. Let them go. Delight in repurposing, donating, selling, and recycling what you can, and send them off with love. Clothes that no longer fit can be let go. You can easily attract new, well-fitting, beautiful clothes any time you decide. Allow yourself to step into joy while you work. Whether it's hours at a time or only a few minutes, do it each day.

Lightening Up So It's Easier

I discovered that choosing a funny name for clutter made me laugh and feel lighter and less serious and burdened by it. It became easier to get into a rhythm once started. I also put on an audiobook that I love to help me to stay light. Perhaps you love music and would benefit from listening to your favourite songs while you work. Or an inspirational podcast or video. Franziska Siragusa recommends, in her wonderful book, *Feng Shui with Archangels, Unicorns, and Dragons*, connecting with the angel of your home to overlight the transformation and help you to make your space a very high-frequency one.

Grounding and the Difficulties of Being Ungrounded

When a person isn't grounded they are drifting around, not quite touching the earth in their energy body. It's hard living this way. If you have had a very sudden spiritual awakening then you might know what it is to be severely ungrounded. I have witnessed the very worst cases where someone has come right out of their body and into fear, resulting in mental illness states. By teaching people how to ground themselves, many mental illnesses could be avoided as they are characterized by being in the head and out of the body.

Psychologists are beginning to recognize how some people are immersive daydreamers and have trouble grounding themselves, or worse, maladaptive daydreamers, where it's hard to be in the real world at all. Being ungrounded is uncomfortable. Thoughts can be racing or flighty. You're not sure what action to take and it's hard to finish what you started. You might be daydreamy, and wonder how you reached your destination as you don't remember any of the journey. You came to this planet to get the full experience. Being grounded is part of the full experience.

Grounding Makes Decluttering Easier

Grounding will help you to declutter—and decluttering will also ground you. Win/win. Start by really connecting with the environment you are in. Feeling your feet on the floor, or your body in the chair. Connect with your body. Rub and/or pat your legs, your back, your tummy, your head. Touch your feet if you can. Be in your body.

Angels, how do I ground myself?

Ask yourself what your body needs right now to ground you.
Send your roots down to the heart of Mother Earth and ask also
for her wisdom. As you declutter, so will you
become more grounded.

Visualizing thick, golden energy roots growing out from the soles of your feet and stretching into the Earth below is a useful visualization to do if you want to feel grounded. But there are many ways. Washing the dishes or housework generally, where your focus is on the spaces below the head. Using larger muscle groups required, for example, when washing windows or washing a vehicle. Activities that bring you back into your body.

Gardening

I was very fortunate to have just bought a polytunnel right before the pandemic in 2020. So when we had that first lockdown I was frequently found either gardening or sunbathing in my polytunnel. I felt so fortunate and believe my angels must have given me a push that winter to get it installed when I did. I discovered the joy of having your hands in the soil and understanding the soil as a living thing and how to feed and nourish it; of watching seeds grow and then plants. This is very grounding too—and 2020 was an "ungrounding" year for many with all that went on with the pandemic and lockdown.

Archangels Sandalphon and Gabriel can help us to learn this important lesson of grounding. Call them in to support you and try out a grounding exercise. As well as the grounding yoga poses, there are also *mudras*—hand positions that help with grounding—that you can learn. Hematite crystal and most black crystals such as obsidian and tourmaline are helpful and you can wear them, keep them in your pocket, or create a grounding crystal grid to work with you remotely.

Drumming is another way to ground yourself. Feel the beat go right through your body. Feel the vibrations. Your beautiful body is the vehicle you chose for this lifetime, this incarnation on this wonderful planet. Enjoy being in your body. And if you have issues with your body, seek healing for this.

Dedicate a Crystal Grid to Your Home

Choose a selection of crystals that appeal to you. You can make simple crystal grids even if you only have one you can work with it. If you have just one, choose something else like shells, stones, or other items from nature (asking their permission first). When I'm on a beach or in a forest, if I ever see something I'd like to take, which is rare nowadays, I ask permission and if it feels okay then I'll take it. I often think what we find in nature belongs in nature except in special circumstances. Feel free to put things back afterwards if this also resonates with you.

One example might be a rose quartz heart at the centre, symbolizing a home full of love. Then a circle around this of citrine crystals for joyfulness and abundance. Then a larger circle around these using base chakra crystals such as tourmaline for tidiness, groundedness, and protection.

Making a Crystal Grid

1. Hold each chosen crystal in your hand in turn, and place it on your heart and on your third eye.

2. Connect it with your base chakra by holding it in your lap and imagining the base chakra opening and connecting with the crystal. Set the intention to dedicate the crystal to your home.

3. See your home as pure and clear in its energy. Everything looks tidy and organized. Your heart leaps with joy when you walk in the front door and into each room. People feel peaceful and energized when they come into your home.

4. Now place the crystal(s) and items in a formation as you are guided. You might like to have them in a circle, or a circle with layers, or a spiral. Allow the crystals to prompt you where to place them.

5. Light a candle and ask the grid to now activate, setting your intention, such as "Please help my home to be tidy and filled with loving energy."

6. Leave them this way for as long as seems appropriate. Feel free to move them slightly, or arrange them differently. Light a candle and connect with your crystal grid, remembering its intention.

7. Thank the crystals for their help with your home.

Getting Others to Help

If you live with other people, does some of the issue lie with others in the home who don't pick up after themselves? Are you being overwhelmed or not knowing what to do with other people's things? What do you say to yourself in your head about this? If you find yourself saying negative, limiting things, this is what you are attracting. Remember to choose your tone and words with care. When someone asks us to do something for them, we are more likely to do it if they use a kind but confident voice that invites us to agree.

Imagine the tidying is already done and then work your way backwards. Ask, *Angels, what did I do to get the help?*

In the case of small children, as well as older children and teens, think about how you might make this part of the routine. Of what's expected in the home. For little ones, they might not be the best help at first but could enjoy tidy-up games that lay the foundations for them as they get older. Know when to delegate also—so, if you are in a position to get somebody in to help even for a couple of hours a week, then maybe this will make a big difference to you.

Your home and the space you reside in is your temple, even if you want to move. See Chapter 6, page 63, for some tips on this.

Behaviour Change
in 111 Seconds

Is there something you are doing that you wish you didn't? A habit or a behaviour that you would love to stop, or replace with something healthier? For most of us humans, there is. And usually more than one thing. This chapter is not meant to replace professional help or support if you need it, but rather to inspire you to work with the angels as well or instead if this is something you can manage without traditional inputs. I also want to share the 111-second "new beginnings" timer with you as a tool to facilitate new beginnings. It can also be used to start a new behaviour.

I'm going to give some common examples here of behaviours that people want to change and how you might go about bringing in the angels to help with these.

What Do You Want to Change and Why?

Write down any behaviours that you do (or don't do), the alternative you'd like to see, and why you'd like to see this change. This helps you to get clear. If you are struggling, keep coming back to the why. You might list one or several reasons that begin with "because." Here are some examples:

- I would like to stop eating junk food in the evenings and instead enjoy a nice hot drink or just relax and read my book/do yoga/insert other health-affirming activities.
  BECAUSE my body feels cluttered when I consume all those calories and I want to feel ease and grace in my body.

- I would like to exercise at least five days a week.
  BECAUSE my body, mind, and energy feel great after exercising.

- I would like to put my phone away and instead read a lot more.
  BECAUSE spending lots of time on my phone doesn't feel good and I really love reading.

- I would like to stop drinking alcohol and instead enjoy soft drinks or water.
  BECAUSE alcohol makes me feel anxious and interferes with my sleep and I love to feel calm, confident, and relaxed.

- I would like to start/continue this project instead of procrastinating.
  BECAUSE I feel upset that I keep putting it off and in my heart it feels good to me to do this.

- I would like to stop smoking/vaping and feel calm and manage stress and situations where I would normally smoke/vape.
  BECAUSE I don't like feeling out of breath when I climb the stairs or the health warnings about smoking/vaping and I love to feel good in my body.

- I would like to stop this negative self-talk and think and speak about myself with kindness and love.
  BECAUSE I know everything can improve in my life if I can forgive/befriend myself.

Remember when you want to stop doing something, it's useful to think of what you'd like to be doing instead. For a smoker, if you didn't smoke, what might you use that time, money, and energy for instead?

Start with One

Again, I would recommend choosing one behaviour to start with. You might have a few you want to change, but check in and see if this will be overwhelming and lead to failure or whether you think it's possible. Only you will know this.

Using the 111 Timer to Stop a Behaviour

Set your timer to 1 minute and 51 seconds, which equals 111 seconds. 111 is a number of new beginnings. Cravings or impulses pass very quickly, much faster than most of us realize. So if there is a behaviour you would like to give up or you have a craving for whatever it is, take out your timer for 111 seconds and give yourself this much time to make an informed decision about whether you really want to do that thing or not. The timer is not there to stop you but to give you a chance to think. You can still, and may well decide to, do the thing after the time is up. But at least you know it wasn't a knee-jerk automatic behaviour where you were acting like an automaton, responding to a craving without giving it some thought.

While the timer is on you have lots of choices about what you might use this time for, just make it count. You might like to:

- Ask the angels a powerful question related to this issue, and write down their answer, taking your time to hear all of the message.

- Practise some *pranayama* (yogic breathing), or simply being aware of the breath.

- Stand in tadasana (mountain pose) to ground yourself and take some nice, calm breaths.

- Practise mindfulness of the thoughts, becoming the watcher, noticing each thought that arises, where it starts and ends, and the next thought that comes along, without judging. Some people like to imagine the thoughts are written on leaves and are passing by down the stream. Or that the thoughts are written on the placards of a marching band, and you watch each marcher go by, seeing the thought passing by.

- Pick an angel card.

- List all the reasons why you want to choose a new behaviour instead of the old one—even better while tapping.

- List all the things you are grateful for in this moment now.

- Say an angel prayer or affirmation(s) of your choice.

- Say a forgiveness decree to yourself, and anyone else, that relates to the behaviour (an example of a forgiveness decree is seen in the Huna Prayer on page 199).

- Do some Angel EFT. You could use the word "release," for example. Or, "Archangel Raphael, help me to release," as Archangel Raphael helps us to release addictions.

- Massage your feet.

- Put beautiful-smelling oils on your pulse points.

- Apply hand cream, taking your time to rub it all in with kindness and luxury.

You could ask: *Angels, how do I maintain healthy eating throughout the day?*

Take some time to plan out what you might like to eat. Make some healthy, high-vibrational snacks that you'll have in stock at the ready if you feel hungry after mealtimes. Use the 111 timer.

Additional Ways to Use the 111 Timer

If it's not that you want to stop, but to start doing something that you've been putting off, the 111 timer is also your friend. Set the timer and, while it's on, do all you can towards the new thing. Make a game of it. Maybe you can even get it done in this time, or you can ready yourself. For example, if it's exercise you want to do, use the time to get your workout clothes on, ready the space, make a phone call, or send an email to book yourself into a class. If you want to write, use the time to get a pen/paper/laptop set up. Light a candle ready for your meditation. Get a bag ready to put clothes into for decluttering. There is a lot you can do in 111 seconds—you might be surprised.

The Seconds as Steps

Think of each of the 111 seconds as a golden step that brings you towards something wonderful, whether it's freedom from an undesirable behaviour or a new habit you know will make your life more fulfilling and richer.

111 Golden Steps Visualization

1. Close your eyes, be aware of your breathing, and ask the angels to help you to ground yourself.

2. Count slowly from 1 all the way to 111. Seconds will be too fast for this exercise. Imagine that each number is a golden step of a great, glowing staircase. At the top of the staircase is a beautiful room or open space in nature that represents your success.

3. When you reach the top, imagine you are free. The angels celebrate your freedom and Archangel Mary is approaching you with a gift. Receive the gift and know that it will help you to maintain your freedom.

4. Thank the angels and allow yourself to come fully back into your body, bringing your newfound freedom and success with you.

Family Connections and Loyalty

Sometimes patterns pass down the family lineage, in the cells, in the DNA, because they haven't been resolved and so they must pass on. Also, we can feel trapped in a habit or behaviour because we worry that by overcoming it we will somehow upset someone in the family. Perhaps a spouse or family member might get jealous or upset if we successfully overcome this problem that they still suffer with. Interestingly, this so-called loyalty can even occur when a loved one or family member has died. If this sounds familiar, ask the angels to help you to let go of this.

George was overweight all his life but, approaching 40, he'd joined a gym and started a programme and was losing weight very successfully. He felt great. But as he approached his goal weight he began to feel troubled and found the old binging behaviours returning. He told me, "I feel like I'm letting Dad down somehow. It's so odd." His father had died three years previously from a heart attack and had always been overweight. George missed him very much. After a meditation with the angels, he asked the question, "Angels, would it upset Dad if I lose this weight?" His experience was profound and beautiful. His face changed and tears filled his eyes. He told me he could see his dad standing in front of him with an angel on either side. His dad told him he would be thrilled for him to lose weight and wanted him to experience health and happiness. This shifted the block and George treasured this memory of his loving father encouraging him to succeed and be fit and healthy.

Anchoring Your Vision for Success

An additional exercise is to regularly imagine situations where you are doing the new behaviour. Especially think up circumstances that have always presented the most challenge. The trigger situations. See yourself managing perfectly, with a big smile, feeling absolutely great. Doing this regularly creates and anchors a strong picture of your success for your third eye. When you can see in your mind and imagine what it looks like, you can feel it. Allow yourself to get excited about it. Say out loud,

"I'm SO happy that…"

Challenge the Old Way of Thinking

The above exercise may offer opportunities to challenge old, unhelpful beliefs. For example, maybe you want to change or stop a behaviour but the idea of not doing whatever it is on holiday/at certain functions/with a particular person seems unthinkable. Ask yourself, what would it be like to be really happy in those situations without doing the behaviour? Challenge yourself to a new way of thinking.

> Ask: *Angels, how can I feel free from worry and fully detach from this behaviour?*

Note what comes up and, if there are any action steps, make sure to take them.

Huna Prayers

A Huna prayer is a very powerful prayer to the universe that you say each day for a specific length of time. I am going to provide some sample templates here that you might like to use, be inspired to create your own, or adjust to suit yourself. Work with your higher self and angelic team when creating or choosing a Huna prayer. And even if there are several you would like to use, use one at a time and consider leaving a gap before starting another.

Is What You Are Asking for the Highest Good?

We don't always know what is for our highest good, but we do know if what we are asking comes from a third-dimensional place. For example, wanting to manifest something to outdo another. If we create a Huna prayer that comes from the wrong place, the angels and masters simply step back. If you aren't sure what you are asking is for the highest good—after all, only the angelic realms really know this—we can trust that what we are requesting or something even better will come to us. Whatever is in perfect divine alignment.

You will notice that there are different ways of phrasing your Huna prayer. You may or may not decide to include the forgiveness aspect, for example. Do what resonates with you. Choose angels, ascended masters, or any angelic beings that appeal to you and your request. Keep your words positive and focused on what you want, not on what you don't want.

Light a candle and create a sacred space for your prayer. Repeat daily for 30 days. If you choose a particular time of day it may be easier to remember.

Huna Prayer to Raise your Baseline Frequency to Feel Better on All Levels

I now forgive anyone who has ever hurt or harmed me, consciously or unconsciously, in this life or any other, in this universe, plane, level, or dimension or any other.
I offer them Grace.
I ask forgiveness for anything I have ever done to hurt or harm anyone, consciously or unconsciously, in this life or any other, in this universe, plane, level, or any other.
I ask for Grace.
I now forgive myself for anything I have ever done to hurt or harm myself or any other, consciously or unconsciously, in this life or any other, in this universe, plane, level, or dimension or any other.
I accept Grace.

Beloved Source, Archangel Metatron,
Masters Quan Yin and St Germain,
In the name of Christ, I ask and humbly pray for assistance in raising my vibration and anchoring it in the higher states for the good of all. I ask that I wake up each morning open to joy and wonderful possibilities so that I feel good on all levels.

[Say the above part three times]

Beloved subconscious mind I hereby ask you to take this prayer with all the energy needed to bring it to reality to Source through my Monad.

Lord, let the rain of blessings fall.

Huna Prayer to Help Animals

[You can choose a specific animal or situation or use this broad-spectrum prayer that acknowledges the New Golden Age, where everyone treats animals kindly and with respect.]

Dear Archangel Fhelyai and Green Dragons,
I, [say your full name] humbly ask and pray from the centre of my being for your divine assistance to help animals everywhere. Please help raise the consciousness of humans all over the planet so that animals are treated kindly and with respect. Help me to hold the vision that this is so
to support my prayer.
I open myself to any way that I can help now that is in alignment with my soul mission.
In the name of Beloved Source, I fully open myself to the vision of animals everywhere being treated with understanding and fairness as human consciousness is raised in alignment with the New Golden Age.
Thank you.

My beloved subconscious mind, I hereby ask and lovingly command that you take this thought-form prayer to Highest Source, along with my fully activated Power of Manifestation.
And so it is.

[Hold the vision of delivering this prayer to Archangel Fhelyai and the Green Dragons for fifteen seconds.]
Highest Source, Love and Light, let the rain of blessings fall.

Huna Prayer for Physical Health

*I now forgive anyone who has ever hurt or harmed me,
consciously or unconsciously, in this life or any other, in this
universe, plane, level, or dimension or any other.
I offer them Grace.
I ask forgiveness for anything I have ever done to hurt or
harm anyone, consciously or unconsciously, in this life or any
other, in this universe, plane, level, or any other.
I ask for Grace.
I now forgive myself for anything I have ever done to hurt
of harm myself or any other, consciously or unconsciously,
in this life or any other, in this universe, plane, level, or
dimension or any other.
I accept Grace.*

*Beloved Source, Archangel Raphael,
and Master Hilarion,
In the name of Christ, I ask and humbly pray for assistance
in healing my body now. I ask that I easily visualize myself
enjoying vibrant physical health on all levels and that my
body follows my vision.*

[Say the above part three times]

*Beloved subconscious mind, I hereby ask you to take this
prayer, with all the energy needed to bring it to reality, to
Source through my Monad. Amen.
And So It Is.*

Dear Source, let the rain of blessings fall.

Huna Prayer for Weight Loss to Reduce Overeating and Increase Exercise

Dear Master Rakoczy and Highest Source Love,
I, [say your full name] humbly ask and pray from the centre of my being for your divine guidance and inspiration to realize a healthy, light, radiant body.
I open myself to immediate inspiration to eat healthy, high-vibrational foods and to exercise in a way that benefits my body perfectly. I ask your wise and loving counsel in maintaining this.
In the name of Beloved Source, I fully open myself to my limitless power of manifestation in having a healthy, happy physical body to assist me to serve on my Source Mission.
I open myself to enlightened images and thoughts about myself at a healthy body weight that lovingly imprints on my being. SO BE IT.

My beloved subconscious mind, I hereby ask and lovingly command that you take this thought-form prayer to Highest Source, along with my fully activated power of manifestation.

[Breathe this prayer to Master Rakoczy and Highest Source for fifteen seconds.]
Highest Source, Love, and Light,
I am open and willing to receive my Blessings.

Huna Prayer to Attract a Wonderful Loving Partner

I now forgive anyone who has ever hurt or harmed me, consciously or unconsciously, in this life or any other, in this universe, plane, level, or dimension or any other.
I offer them, Grace.
I ask forgiveness for anything I have ever done to hurt or harm anyone, consciously or unconsciously, in this life or any other, in this universe, plane, level, or any other.
I ask for Grace.
I now forgive myself for anything I have ever done to hurt or harm myself or any other, consciously or unconsciously, in this life or any other, in this universe, plane, level, or dimension or any other. I accept Grace.

Beloved Source, Archangel Chamuel, and Lady Master Quan Yin,
In the name of all that is light, I ask and humbly pray for assistance in attracting a wonderful, loving partner now. I open myself to new opportunities to meet this person if I have not already, and easily create and imprint my vision of being in a joyful relationship, which helps me to quickly manifest this into reality. I am receptive to your signs, prompts, and guidance. With all my heart and being, I am attracting a partner with the following qualities: [name what qualities you would love in your new partner]. *And so it is. Beloved subconscious mind, please take this request through my higher self and my Monad to Source. My vision is now anchored.*
[Place your hands on your heart centre and breathe your vision, seeing Archangel Chamuel and Quan Yin pouring light over you and into your heart, which is expanding with much light now.]
I open myself fully to this now.

Huna Prayer to Help Mother Earth

Dear Archangel Purlimiek and the Lemurian Angels,
Dragons, and Crystals,
I now forgive all those who have caused harm to Mother
Earth in the present day and throughout history. From the
deepest and wisest part of my I Am presence,
I offer them grace.
I ask forgiveness for the harm I have caused Mother Earth in
my life and from the whole of my being,
I ask for grace.
I forgive myself for the harm I have caused our Mother Earth
and through my soul and Monad,
I accept grace.

Please help raise the consciousness of all humans now so
that excellent care is taken of our planet. I ask that wonderful
solutions arise now to heal the damages done and to prevent
any further harm from occurring. That humans, remembering
our true nature, live gently and blissfully on Mother Earth,
our exquisite home and that all of nature can thrive and live
in harmony and delight. And So It Is.

[Release this prayer from the heart of your being into a ball
of sparkling golden-white light and see it being received by
Archangel Purlimiek and the Lemurian Angels,
Dragons, and Crystals.]
Source and Highest Light, I accept the blessings now and feel
them raining down on Mother Earth and
all of her inhabitants.

Other Huna Prayer Ideas

For manifesting more money; attracting the perfect new job; helping your child; to stop and prevent war and conflict and speed peace and harmony; to help your country/city/village grow more of their own organic food; to support bees and pollinators; to heal your heart; learning the lessons your body is showing you; to help raise the consciousness of all those in positions of power in your country or in the world; to support the animal kingdom; to help homeless people; to clean the oceans; to heal your inner child. The possibilities are endless.

28

The Rainbow Fire
of Source

I received the Rainbow Fire of Source when I began working with Merlin and the Rainbow Dragons. When you work with this energy you can transmute the old and powerfully manifest the new. Come into alignment with your soul journey and highest light.

I was given the following decree:

I Am The Rainbow Fire of Source
I Am Archangel Metatron
I Am Merlin
I Am The Shekinah
I Am Divine Manifestation
I Am Infinite Source Light

Try saying this I Am decree three times for eleven days, and see what changes in your life.

The Rainbow Dragons

Work with these vibrant beings to bring more wonder into your life. Whenever I see a rainbow I feel huge joy, and I understand rainbows and rainbow light as my sign from the universe that love is everywhere and that we are an integral part of this love and magic. Do you have a symbol like this, that fills you with delight? If you don't, ask the angels what yours is.

Rainbow dragons can immediately lift the heaviness and clear the cobwebs. They bring in new possibilities and fresh ideas. Open doors where things feel stuck. Call upon the rainbow dragons to lift your heart when you're feeling weighed down or overwhelmed. Ask them to bring magic into your relationships, or to help you to attract new friendships or a partner. Ask them to assist you in manifesting money and in transforming unhelpful beliefs and patterns about prosperity or lack. Ask them to bless your food and help you to make good choices for your body. Work with them when you are physically cleaning or energetically clearing a place.

Unusually for dragons, the rainbow dragons embody all of the four elements—water, because water is needed to create rainbows; fire, because the fire of the sun (light) is also required; earth, because the rainbow appears to be touching the earth; and air because it appears in the air. When I learned about the dragons I was guided to connect with my own personal dragon. I saw a dragon of every colour approaching me. He told me he was a rainbow dragon. Later, he told me about the Rainbow Fire of Source and how to invoke it very powerfully with the decree I have included above.

This came to me very quickly, all in one go. And I was guided to write about it in a blog and lead people through an attunement to the Rainbow Fire of Source. Use this powerful fire to co-create things for the highest good with these divinities. Merlin is one of my guides and he helps me to remember that the world is full of magic and that we are a part of the fabric of that magic. One day some years ago I was in England, driving to Glastonbury, and my heart soared as the iconic Tor came into view. I thought to myself, "I wonder why I love this place so much and feel compelled to keep coming here." Instantly, Merlin replied, "I bring you here." This made me laugh. It was all the information I needed.

Merlin, The Shekinah, and Archangel Metatron

Merlin is a dragon master and has had many powerful incarnations, including St Germain and Abraham, and he is well known for his assistance with King Arthur of Avalon. Master Merlin takes the form of a mage, wizard, alchemist, shapeshifter, and superb, dazzling light being who can assist you if you work with him. As he was St Germain in one of his incarnations, he is also connected to the violet flame and helps us to transmute lower energies.

Merlin says, "Be bold and remember who you are. Let no one disempower you for your place in the universe is an important one. The earth under your feet is filled with magic and healing. The air around you is bursting with light and inspiration. Connect with nature and trees to activate your inner mage, who awaits you now. Magic is everywhere if you only look."

The Shekinah, the feminine aspect of Archangel Metatron's higher light, is the universal energy that created our world and embodies pure, creative vision. You can tap into this potent energy via the Rainbow Fire of Source, or by inviting it. The Shekinah reminds you of your important role in this incarnation and in the cosmos. Work with this energy to command forth your true essence as it supports you on your mission. It will give you courage and help you to remember your divine immortality.

I asked to connect with the Shekinah and I felt like a cloak of light was placed around me. There was a slight humming in my brain, as though I was being attuned to divine light. My whole body felt as though it was being infused in sparkling light, and all the petals of my heart chakra opened wide. I was aware of little chakras in my hands lighting up. It was exquisite.

Archangel Metatron governs the stellar gateway chakra and oversees our ascension process. Ask him to bring the Metatron cube, down through your 12 fifth-dimensional chakras to clear them and fill them with its vast light.

Meet Master Merlin Visualization

1. Your unicorn is approaching you. Make eye contact and feel the love she communicates to you.

2. She wants to bring you on a journey. Sit up on her back as she soars into the air and travels through the dimensions.

3. She brings you to a beautiful hill surrounded by rolling countryside with layers of mist. You are in the magical land of Avalon, the sun is setting and the moon is rising. Note the phase of the moon, for this reflects your phase right now. Is it waxing or waning?

4. At the top of the hill is the iconic roofless tower of St Michael, its stones transformed to crystals, and from its archway emerges Merlin. He has been expecting you. His own brilliant silver-white unicorn waits with your unicorn.

5. Merlin holds a great staff of light that has a glowing tip. He raises it up, pointing the glowing tip in front of your third eye, removing one of the veils. You can see things more clearly now. There is magic everywhere, and you are lighting up with joy and inspiration.

6. Merlin places his staff in front of him and it stands upright all by itself. He looks at it intently and his eyes glow silver and blue and another staff, almost exactly like it, appears by its side. He hands you this new one. What colour is it? How does it feel? What qualities does it have?

7. Tell Merlin how you would like to work with him. Is there something you would like to transmute in your life? Or do you just want more magic and to remember your loving powers? Are you seeking something? He listens carefully. Receive any information he gives you.

8. You step outside of the tower and you feel the strong pulsating of a huge crystal that sits under the earth of the Tor, the hill you are on. You gaze at the beautiful land of Avalon around you, and see there is a lake below surrounding the Tor, sparkling silver.

9. You walk down the steps with Merlin, bringing your staff, and the unicorns walk alongside you.

10. Merlin shows you your own boat that is moored and waiting for you. Sit in the boat. Merlin comes with you and together you take a trip around the lake. You get to see the Tor from all angles and its beauty is breathtaking. Merlin is telling you all about the powers you have that you have forgotten. He reminds you of your magical self. You tell him about some earthly situations and, for each one, he tells you how you might use your magic to help with this. Take your time.

11. When you return you feel lighter, and you get back onto land, where your unicorn is waiting for you. Look back up at the tower and allow yourself to absorb all the light you need. Now your unicorn is taking you back through the dimensions to where you started.

Manifest with the Rainbow Fire of Source

1. Place your hands, palms facing one another, either side of your heart space.

2. Focus on something very dear to you that you would like to manifest.

3. Trust completely that it will come if it is for your highest good. And that if it is not for the highest good, something even better will come your way.

4. Now see it, having manifested and hold this image and all the good feelings between your hands in a bubble of light that is being created.

5. Invoke the Rainbow Fire of Source by saying or singing the following I AM invocation three times, but in between each time saying thank you Master Merlin, Rainbow Dragons, and Angels for . . . (name what it is you would like to manifest as though it is already here). So you will say the thank you part twice and the I AM part three times:

   I AM The Rainbow Fire of Source

   I AM Archangel Metatron

I AM Merlin

I AM The Shekinah

I AM Divine Manifestation

I AM Infinite Source Light

"Thank you, Master Merlin, Rainbow Dragons, Archangel Metatron, and The Shekinah for . . ."

6. Feel a bubble of Rainbow Fire between your hands that surrounds your manifestation request. Hold it here and feel it being energized by the fire.

7. Merlin, Archangel Metatron, The Shekinah, and Infinite Source Light are with you. See the Rainbow Dragons swirling around too, blowing their Rainbow Fire over you and your wish.

8. Tune in to your vision of this being already manifested, and ask your future self if they have any advice for you now in terms of what to do next to support this in its creation process.

9. Now blow it away, up to Source. Release it. The Rainbow Dragons are bringing it to Source. Source shines the Rainbow Fire down over you as a shower of blessings; feel it coming through your entire fifth-dimensional chakra system. Your chakras are all lighting up with your vision as though it is already in place, and the wisdom needed to manifest it.

10. Thank the Rainbow Fire of Source, Master Merlin, Archangel Metatron, the Rainbow Dragons, The Shekinah, Source, and your divinity. Trust that It Is Done.

11. Write down any insights or action steps that have come to you and be open to more ideas dropping into your mind, and doors of opportunity related to your request opening.

And Now...

What we do after a visualization is important. I like to think of it as anchoring the information and guidance obtained from the spiritual realms in our everyday reality. Remember to think of the physical—we have been working with the third-eye chakra and the higher realms, and to ground this spiritual work into the physical we need to take physical action.

- What can you do with your hands and your feet to make your dream come true?
- What steps could you take today?
- What do you need to put in place to help yourself to complete this next step?

The Rainbow Fire of Source can support you on many levels. It is very earthy and can bring you the energy to step into your body and physically undertake the steps you need to create your vision. Ask it to blow away procrastination and all of its aspects and help you to have a diamond focus on bringing about what it is you want.

Rainbow Fire of Source, what is my next step?

Productivity –
The Angels as Coaches

I like to think of the angels as loving and supportive coaches, and I created a workshop called *Angel Coach* to share this idea. How does a benevolent, supportive coach operate? They tease out of you your goals and motivations, and assist you in making a plan and finding your strengths so that you have the best chance of success. They are non-judgemental and want what's for your highest good. When things aren't going to plan, they help you to see around obstacles and make adjustments accordingly. The angels are like this too, and to "employ" them we just need to ask.

Favourite Tools for Overcoming Procrastination

Angel EFT to Shift Energy Blocks to Procrastination

1. Call in an angel, archangel, or loving angelic being to support you to get this thing done.

2. Use Angel EFT, setting the intention to clear away any blocks to you getting this done.

3. Take one small action and see where it leads you.

Pomodoro Technique

I recommend, from my own experience, using the 25-minute method or Pomodoro Technique. I use this for any number of things—even writing this book I set my timer for 25 minutes because I enjoy writing for short chunks of time. The Pomodoro is a time management method developed by Francesco Cirillo in the late 1980s. Here, you work on a task for 25 minutes, then take a break, then do another 25 minutes. This has helped me hugely. I find putting the timer on has the spectacular effect of stopping me from overthinking and just getting on with it.

If you don't have 25 minutes, choose a shorter amount of time, and set your alarm to go off when the time is up so you don't have to keep checking. During this time, set the intention to give your whole attention to the task at hand. If something interrupts you for any reason, try to pause the timer and resume afterwards.

The Five-Second Rule

Mel Robbins' five-second rule is another helpful technique for overcoming any sort of procrastination. Mel says that by saying, "5, 4, 3, 2, 1" you can propel yourself into action without the mind getting in the way. Try it; it's a bit like a rocket taking off. Use it to get out of bed, get into your exercise clothes, get out for a walk, make that difficult phone call, start that email, apologize *anyway*, sort those clothes . . . and the list goes on.

Visualizing the End Result and Manifestation Tapping

Visualizing the end result is another incredibly useful way to launch yourself into action. Imagine that you have already done the thing that you have been avoiding. It's complete, or at least you have achieved what you can imagine. By the end of the year, the month, the week, the day, the hour, the next five minutes.

If it's a large task, use many different time points, starting from the end result and working backwards. It helps us to be able to imagine what we're moving towards. And if you're not sure what the end result looks like, instead tune in to the feeling. The relief, the joy, the celebration, the peace. I used this for a presentation I was nervous about, and I combined imagining the end result with tapping. I call this Manifestation Tapping—just like the video I share on "tapping to manifest a holiday."

Step by Step

Sometimes we overwhelm ourselves by looking too far ahead with the steps we need to take. Big achievements happen through showing up, again and again. If you dwell too much on how to face the enormous goal, it can feel totally overwhelming. Angels remind us that we only need to take the next step. The step after that will become clear when we've done that. There's no need to jump ahead with the steps. It doesn't work that way.

The same principle works for saving money, losing weight, manifesting something, improving your relationship, creating a collection of artwork . . . Start by uncovering the next step, and take it.

As always, ask questions: "Angels, how can I get on and do this today? What might be the best first step?"

Meditation and Picking an Oracle Card

Meditation, picking an angel card, or anything that helps you to connect with your higher self will also assist you in thinking positively, which helps motivate you in resetting negative thoughts. Take a few minutes to light a candle, and sit at an altar or space you have kept aside for your oracle cards or candle or anything that symbolizes connecting with angels to you. Close your eyes and open your heart to your highest wisdom. Imagine you are surrounded by angels and other loving, high-frequency beings of light. They all want to help and support you. Tell them about your intentions, and about any struggles. What message do they bring?

Making a List

I love using lists, both digital and handwritten. I can check in with it, and I learned over time not to put too much on my list as that can lead to more procrastination. The list has to be doable or just about doable so that it pushes you. And I don't get cross with myself for not doing everything on the list, instead, I ask questions. Why didn't I get that done? That's interesting, perhaps I need to change it, get some help, or take it off.

Writers and Procrastination

As a writer, I want to share this with the writers and prospective writers out there. Prolific bestselling author Stephen King shares the insight about writers: Some of us wait around for the muse and the rest of us get to work.

I used to suffer from procrastination about writing. It could be painful as I was very critical about my work and had to learn about the power of letting myself write anything at all and then editing it afterwards, letting energy build and flow. I am so grateful to know this now and wish this for all writers everywhere.

Out of Head and Onto Page

A blank sheet of paper to write down all your ideas is also a lovely way to get thoughts out of your head and onto the page. Let yourself run free, writing down any silly or brilliant idea that pops into your head. You can sort them out later.

Balancing Masculine and Feminine Energies

Remember to balance your masculine and feminine energies. If you found the title of this chapter appealing, you might be what some people call a *do-er*: someone who loves to get things done, has a list of stuff to accomplish and likes to stay on track. Or maybe you aspire to this. Either way, remember that this is a typically masculine way of being. Which is great, as long as you also embody your feminine way of being. Receiving. Being, rather than doing.

To activate your feminine energy, go for a walk in nature, and absorb the beauty there. Let it wash over you and clear your energy fields. Listen to a visualization. Lie down in *shavasana* (corpse pose) or reclining goddess for a while. Have a sauna, a massage, a swim, a nap in the daytime, a foot soak . . . you get the idea.

Stay in the Present to Support Powerful Actions

It's good to become aware of your blocks as well as your strengths to learn from and remove them. By that, I do not mean an endless quest of looking back into your past to see why you might not be able to take action. Healing past pain certainly has its place, but my experience both personally and with clients is that dwelling too long in the past and the "reasons" can create a fog of confusion that takes you further away from achieving your goal.

We are complex beings, and there are many possible explanations as to why we behave the way we do. We might never get to the bottom of it. If you feel you cannot begin your dream of watercolour painting because of childhood trauma, then seek help to heal the trauma, but also look to the present. Keep on coming back to what's now. Ask, *Angels, what can I do today to support myself to do the thing I desire?*

The Language You Use Creates Your Experiences

The words we use have a creative force of their own. If we are stuck in procrastination over something, and we keep telling the same story about it, then we are perpetuating the problem.

For example, if you say, "I'd love to have my own small business, selling these . . . or providing . . . ," these are powerful words that attract doors opening for you to do just this. However, if you finish the sentence by saying, "but I never have the time, don't know where to start, am too busy, have no confidence, won't succeed because x, y, or z, am not good with money," you have just slammed the door shut right after opening it. If you believe any of those latter kind of things to be true, acknowledge them but word them in a more supportive "door opening" way.

Examples:
- I'm not good with money/I'm open to learning how to be good with money.
- I'm too busy/I welcome having the time to do this.

- I've no confidence/I'm supporting myself to grow more confident each day.

Note: write down both statements, but then get rid of the first one and keep only the affirming one.

Final Words

Dearest reader, the end brings me back to the beginning again. Ask your angels for everything. They love to help you. Nothing is too big, too small, or too insignificant.

Your light matters, and when you bring the angels in, you shine even brighter.

That benefits everyone. The whole world.

With love and gratitude,
Susan

Exercise Overview

Bibliography

Browne, Susan. *Angel EFT: Tap into the Angelic Realms with Modern Energy EFT.* Eastbourne: Dragon Rising Publishing, 2017.

Byrne, Rhonda. *The Power*. New York: Atria Books, 2014.

Cameron, Julia. *The Artist's Way: A Spiritual Path to Higher Creativity*. New York: TarcherPerigee, 2002.

Carr, Allen. *Allen Carr's Easy Way to Quit Emotional Eating*. London: Arcturus, 2019.

Cooper, Diana. *Dragons: Your Celestial Guardians*. London: Hay House, 2018.
———. *The Golden Future*. New York: Hay House, 2023.
———. *The Magic of Unicorns: Help and Healing from the Heavenly Realms*. London: Hay House, 2020.
———. *The Magic of Unicorns Oracle Cards*. Carlsbad, CA: Hay House, 2021.

Neal's Yard Remedies. *Neal's Yard Remedies Healing Foods: Eat Your Way to a Healthier Life*. London: Dorling Kindersley, 2013.

Robbins, Mel. *The 5-Second Rule*. Brentwood, TN: Flavio Republic, 2017.

Siragusa, Franziska. *Feng Shui with Archangels, Unicorns, and Dragons*. Rochester, VT: Findhorn Press, 2025.

Acknowledgements

With a huge angel energy hug, I thank all my readers, people I've worked with, and those who encourage me by taking the time to read my emails, blogs, and social media posts, and watch my videos. Years ago, I wouldn't have thought these things possible, and it makes me so full of joy to do this work.

As well as my angelic helpers, to whom I am eternally grateful, I would like to thank my agent, Christian Schweiger, who believed in this book when I told him about the idea of it. Many thanks to my writing friends, angel teacher friends at the Diana Cooper School of White Light, Diana Cooper herself, and Anna, Jacqui, Richard, Sabine and all the team at both Findhorn Press and Inner Traditions.

About the Author

Photo by Richard Elliott

Susan Browne is a life coach, author, and the creator of *Angel EFT*, commended by spiritual bestselling author Diana Cooper and tapping wizard Brad Yates. She has guided workshops in personal development and spiritual awakening for more than fifteen years and also teaches creativity and biodiversity classes. A trained mental health nurse and counsellor, she is passionate about mindset and well-being.

As YouTube's Angel EFT Lady, Susan has shared many demonstrational videos and helped clients around the world. An internationally recognized teacher and healer, originally from Warwickshire, UK, Susan lives in County Kerry in Ireland. For more information visit:

https://angeleft.com and **https://www.youtube.com/user/ AngelEFTLady**

FINDHORN PRESS

Life-Changing Books

Learn more about us and our books at
www.findhornpress.com

For information on the Findhorn Foundation:
www.findhorn.org

Scan the QR code and save 25% at InnerTraditions.com.
Browse over 2,000 titles on spirituality, the occult, ancient
mysteries, new science, holistic health, and natural medicine.